EXPERIENCE
BRITISH
COLUMBIA

Published by

PANACHE
P A N A C H E   P A R T N E R S

Panache Partners Canada Inc.
1424 Gables Court
Plano, TX 75075
469.246.6060
Fax: 469.246.6062
www.panache.com

Publishers: Brian G. Carabet and John A. Shand

Printed in Malaysia

Distributed by Independent Publishers Group
800.888.4741

PUBLISHER'S DATA

Experience British Columbia

Library of Congress Control Number: 2010934405

ISBN 13: 978-1-933415-92-5
ISBN 10: 1-933415-92-4

First Printing 2010

10 9 8 7 6 5 4 3 2 1

Right: Vancouver Convention Centre, page 96

Previous Page: Cathedral Mountain Lodge, page 172

This publication is intended to showcase the work of extremely talented
people. The publisher does not require, warrant, endorse, or verify any
professional accreditations, educational backgrounds, or professional
affiliations of the individuals or firms included herein. All copy and
photographs published herein have been reviewed and approved as free
of any usage fees or rights and accurate by the individuals and/or firms
included herein.

Panache Partners, LLC, is dedicated to the restoration and conservation of
the environment. Our books are manufactured with strict adherence to an
environmental management system in accordance with ISO 14001 standards,
including the use of paper from mills certified to derive their products from
well-managed forests. We are committed to continued investigation of
alternative paper products and environmentally responsible manufacturing
processes to ensure the preservation of our fragile planet.

EXPERIENCE
BRITISH
COLUMBIA

Sunshine Coast Tourism, page 115

FOREWORD

Try to find someone who doesn't love British Columbia. It's one of those places where the mere mention is met with an, "Oh, I love it there!" or an, "I've always wanted to visit." It makes living a traveling life that much more connected, to find people all over the world that sigh at the sound of the name of your home. It also makes this collection, *Experience British Columbia*, all the more enticing. It's a perfect invitation to enjoy—from home or in person—all that this uniquely stunning region has to offer.

Victoria, on Vancouver Island, is in my earliest memories—the playing fields of Gordon Head, the lacrosse box at Lambrick Park, the hockey rink in Oak Bay. As I grew up, my friends and I continued to find great places to get outside: swimming in the Sooke Potholes, skiing and sledding at Mount Washington, staring at the amazing old-growth of the Carmanah Valley, and scampering around the coastline rocks and beaches. Wandering among the tide pools was wonder, exploration, adventure, and thrills wrapped into a simple scramble on the shore. Now the island has extensive biking, walking, and hiking trails for anyone to find their own path.

And then you leave Vancouver Island, and the province just opens up in front of you, a tall wall of grandeur that makes you feel small and lucky at the same time. The mountains on the mainland have always been a key part of my training, and if you've ever done the Grouse Grind in North Van, you'll understand why. As I get older, they don't get any kinder, yet my appreciation for them grows every year. From outdoor challenges, to local nonprofits and innovative businesses that are uncovering and addressing true community needs, to the "supernatural" setting that encompasses it all, British Columbia is unsurpassed for its energy and environment.

Coming home for the Vancouver 2010 Winter Olympic Games was the event of a lifetime—how incredible to be representing British Columbia and Canada on that stage, and sharing in it with talents like Sarah McLachlan, Rick Hansen, and my friend Wayne Gretzky. I'm hoping I'll one day be able to fully express to my children what that meant to me—the notion of country, what it is to be part of the global citizenry, what it means to be just one among so many, each with responsibilities and legacies to hopefully fulfill. My foundation's platforms for children are a big part of my connection to the province now, as we work to ensure that all children here have the opportunity to grow up healthy and contribute to their communities.

I wasn't born here, but BC is my home. I hope as you visit—whether for pleasure or business, for a week or a new chapter in life—you'll take a moment to experience even a little of what BC has to offer. Walk through Stanley Park, visit Vancouver Island, or share a pint of homebrew with a friend in the Okanagan. BC is made for memories. And when, recounting yours, you hear that familiar sigh of appreciation or anticipation, know that this BC guy knows just how you feel.

Cheers to a great stay,

Steve Nash

INTRODUCTION

*E*xperiences shape our views of the world and broaden our horizons. A day's excursion close to home, an overnight stay in another city, an extended vacation abroad—all have the ability to open our minds and transform our perspectives.

In *Experience British Columbia*, we track establishments across the province to discover what's unique, revolutionary, innovative, and often life-changing about them. These best of the best entrepreneurs and environmental stewards are what make British Columbia a true destination not to be missed.

Each type of experience has something different to offer. Taken all together, shopping, dining, lodging, relaxing, and fun compose a full understanding of life in BC for both locals and visitors. This book will take you on a voyage across British Columbia, moving from Vancouver Island and the Lower Mainland on the West Coast up further inland to Whistler and over to the Okanagan and beyond. Our carefully curated selection of various experiences is stunningly showcased, presenting a diverse array from each region of the province. ENJOY discovering landmark sights and attractions, APPRECIATE arts and culture, RELAX in style at hotels and spas, INDULGE at popular restaurants and lounges, and SHOP at the finest boutiques and showrooms.

Experience British Columbia is a breathtaking journey through one of Canada's most beautiful provinces, inspiring you to explore the world around you.

Experience life to the fullest. Experience British Columbia.

Vancouver Aquarium, page 95

ENJOY
Sights & Attractions

APPRECIATE
Arts & Culture

CONTENTS

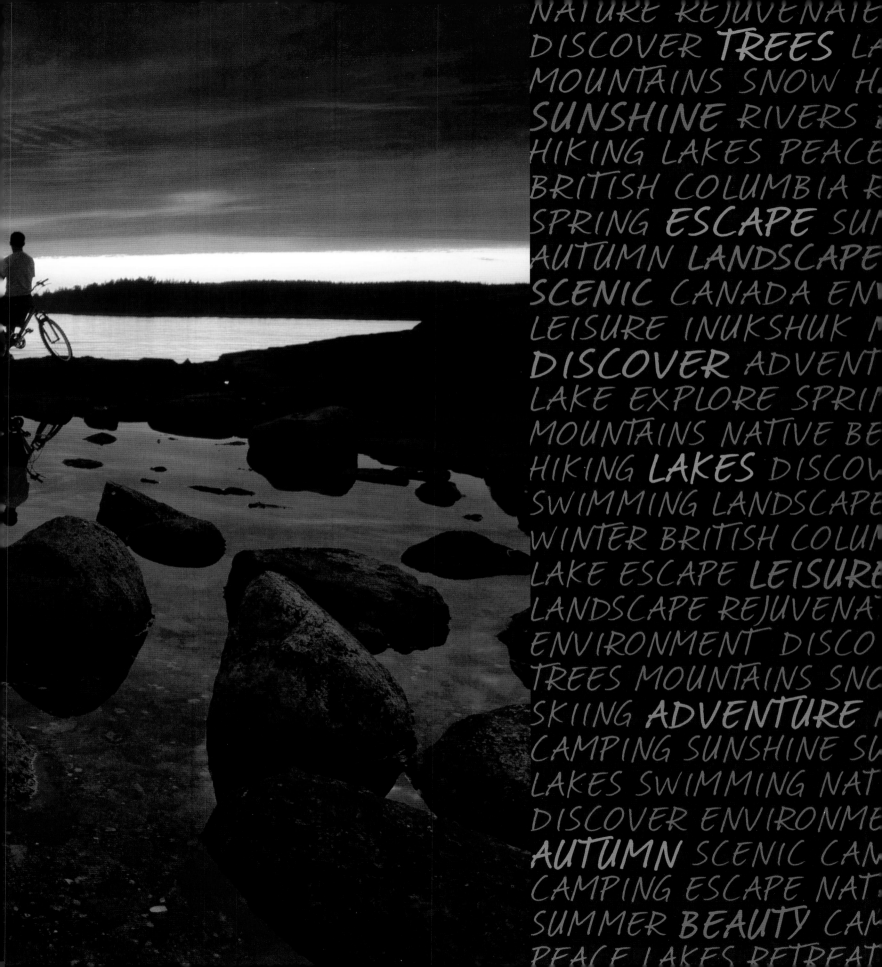

Maple Ridge, page 28

Sunshine Coast Tourism, page 115

Kettle Valley Steam Railway, page 102

Pacific National Exhibition, page 34

Capilano Suspension Bridge, page 59

Vancouver Aquarium, page 95

BC Place, page 54

Sun Peaks Resort, page 106

ENJOY

SIGHTS & ATTRACTIONS

Play. Discover. Move. The pastime of sightseeing marquee attractions and enjoying dazzling sights beckons to travelers of all ages. You'll explore castles, aquariums, and theme parks, tour gorgeous golf courses and athletic facilities, soak up nature at parks, gardens, and lakes, and glean facts from fascinating landmarks and historic sites. Distinctive towns and cities offer irresistible day trip opportunities, exciting outdoor pursuits appeal to thrillseekers, and an array of entertaining transportation options awaits you.

GolfBC Group

Golf is a game of precision, tradition, and intelligence. Burrard International, which has been creating and acquiring premium championship golf destinations in British Columbia since 1990, applies those same qualities to the operation of its 12 courses—nine in British Columbia and three in Hawaii. Assembled into one organization known as the GolfBC Group, this series is the largest group of courses and clubs in Western Canada, a collection of world-class facilities where players can enjoy total golfing excellence.

British Columbia offers many fantastic golf courses, such as the scenic Furry Creek Golf & Country Club, and GolfBC's rank with the best of the best. The province has even received an international stamp of quality—the International Association of Golf Tour Operators selected it as its 2007 "Golf Destination of the Year" for North America as part of its awards. No wonder GolfBC courses have played host to the likes of Jack Nicklaus, Tiger Woods, Arnold Palmer, Michelle Wie, and other top professionals in the sport. Though the playing experience of each course varies, the common themes of exceptional design, remarkable scenery, and superior service run throughout. GolfBC's dedication to providing unique experiences is unmistakable to the resort golfer and enthusiast. Whether in Vancouver, Whistler, the Okanagan, or Vancouver Island, a GolfBC course offers itself a premier choice for golf.

Vancouver
800.446.5322 www.golfbc.com

Photograph by Rob Perry

ARBUTUS RIDGE GOLF CLUB AND OLYMPIC VIEW GOLF CLUB

Golf courses are often thought of as havens of tranquility, peaceful retreats where the mind and body can focus on one single task—most often, keeping the ball out of mischief. At GolfBC's Arbutus Ridge Golf Club, where the green of the "knee-rattling" 17th hole is situated on an island green, adventurous golfers can take advantage of the challenging holes while admiring the charming country setting. Undertaking this sublime journey requires intelligence and the ability to hit a variety of shots. The three finishing holes in particular—declared by locals to be the most difficult finishing holes on Vancouver Island—demand absolute attention.

Located in the seaside community of Cobble Hill and only 10 minutes from the cultural city of Duncan, Arbutus Ridge combines athletic sophistication with rustic allure. The Satellite Channel flows alongside and Mt. Baker stands guard over the 18 holes, which offer some of the most spectacular vistas on Vancouver Island. The genuine service, fabulous scenery, and outstanding layout are just a few reasons why Arbutus Ridge earned a four-star *Golf Digest* rating in 2009. To experience the scenery without the exercise, pay a visit to the glass-fronted clubhouse and take in the mountain and ocean views, or relax on the legendary Satellite Bar & Grille's patio overlooking the 18th hole.

3515 Telegraph Road, Cobble Hill
250.743.5000 www.golfbc.com

It's easy to be seduced by the loveliness of Olympic View Golf Club. Situated within a pristine forest, the course boasts spectacular views of the Olympic Mountains and—thanks to its location on the southernmost tip of Vancouver Island—some of the mildest weather Canada has to offer, facilitating year-round play. But don't think Olympic View is just another pretty face. Underneath its lovely façade is one of the most demanding and exciting courses in all of Canada.

Beginning with the first hole's undulating par 4 and finishing with the deceptive changes in elevation on the 18th, the 6,534 yards of play offer a striking combination of brains and beauty. The 17th hole certainly leaves an impression with its huge rock column, Japanese garden, and 60-foot Hawaiian-esque waterfall that thunders regally beside the green. Another waterfall on the 8th hole and 12 lakes complete the astounding design.

Located just 20 minutes from downtown Victoria, Olympic View offers a fully equipped clubhouse featuring West Coast contemporary cuisine at Forester's Bistro and Bar with floor-to-ceiling windows and a wraparound patio overlooking holes 1, 10, and 18. Outstanding service, astonishing natural beauty, and challenging play are only a few of the reasons this GolfBC championship course is the recipient of numerous awards year after year.

643 Latoria Road, Victoria
250.474.3673 www.golfbc.com

Photographs by Rob Perry

FURRY CREEK GOLF & COUNTRY CLUB AND MAYFAIR LAKES GOLF & COUNTRY CLUB

On the way to Whistler, there exists a magnificent sight that tempts scores of visitors into taking an unplanned detour. Jutting out into the Pacific Ocean inlet is the green of Furry Creek's 14th hole, an emerald peninsula flanked by chalky-white boulders and the sapphire waters of Howe Sound. Built in 1993 from the vision of Robert Muir Graves, GolfBC's Furry Creek Golf & Country Club offers so much natural beauty that it's sometimes hard for golfers to keep their minds on the game.

With challenging features such as a 165-foot drop from tee to green on the first hole, concentration on this course is a must. The 6,025 yards have tested amateurs, professionals, and even fictional characters: Adam Sandler's hockey player-turned-golfer vented his frustrations to television host Bob Barker during a scene filmed here for the 1996 film "Happy Gilmore."

Having been sculpted from a mountainside site that ascends 350 feet from the rocky shore of Howe Sound, Furry Creek's alluring scenery and stimulating surprises make it all but impossible to drive past "the prettiest golf hole in all of British Columbia" without stopping for a round.

150 Country Club Road, Furry Creek
604.896.2224 www.golfbc.com

Eminently playable yet infinitely challenging, Mayfair Lakes is the perfect golf retreat. Featuring water on 13 of its 18 holes, adding as much difficulty as aesthetic appeal, this Les Furber-designed course offers secluded country ambience mere minutes away from downtown Vancouver and its international airport. Impeccable course conditioning, a hallmark of the Mayfair Lakes experience, has won it a well-deserved reputation for uncompromising excellence since it opened in 1989.

As a former host to the BC Tel Open and the Canadian Tour, the course continues to rank as a favorite among local and visiting golfers alike. The 6,641-yard, 18-hole course has also been voted onto *BC Business Magazine*'s "Vancouver's Top Ten Golf Courses" list and been named a

"Best Place to Play" by *Golf Digest*. Accolades aside, it is the picturesque environment and fast, well-protected greens that draws golfers to its links. Coupled with terrific service and impressive views of the North Shore Mountains, Mayfair Lakes is a genuine golf sanctuary.

5460 No. 7 Road, Richmond
604.276.0585 www.golfbc.com

Photographs: above by Henebry; facing page top and center by Rob Perry; facing page bottom courtesy of Furry Creek Golf & Country Club

GALLAGHER'S CANYON GOLF & COUNTRY CLUB AND THE OKANAGAN GOLF CLUB

Gallagher's Canyon is billed as the quintessential Okanagan Valley golf experience: rugged yet refined. After taking in the sweeping blue skies, rocky bluffs, and tall groves of ponderosa pines that frame the immaculately manicured course, the description seems more than appropriate.

Ranked among the top 50 courses in Canada by *SCOREGolf* magazine, the Canyon Course's 18 championship holes, designed by the architectural team of Bill Robinson and Les Furber, offer both robust scenery and superior play. There is also the chance to play one of the finest executive-length nine-hole courses in the province, the 1,984-yard Pinnacle Course, which poses a challenge to any level of golfer.

The GBC Golf Academy at Gallagher's Canyon, featuring a double-ended 300-yard driving range with target greens, bunkers, and chipping and putting areas, is known as one of the finest learning and practice facilities in the province. To refuel after a mentally and physically tiring day on the links, pay a visit to the well-appointed clubhouse, where the culinary team tees up a memorable dining experience using fresh local fruits and vegetables and award-winning wines from the Okanagan Valley.

4320 Gallagher's Drive West, Kelowna
250.861.4240 www.golfbc.com

Bears and quails may seem like an unlikely pairing—unless it's The Bear and The Quail, the two exhilarating courses at GolfBC's Okanagan Golf Club.

With dramatic, sculpted fairways that wind through the sage brush hills of British Columbia's sun-drenched southern interior, The Bear is a marvel of both manmade design and natural harmony with its well-placed bunkers, sculpted fairways, tiered greens, and scenic views of Lake McIvor. The 18-hole, 6,885-yard course created by Nicklaus Designs opened in 1999, and its signature 3rd hole has been testing ambitious players ever since.

The Quail, built in 1994 and designed by the legendary Les Furber, offers nearly 6,800 yards of multi-tiered fairways that meander around a majestic rock bluff. Breathtaking vistas and natural splendor surround every hole, especially the course's signature 18th.

Together, The Bear and The Quail form an irresistible combination, making The Okanagan Golf Club a true destination for connoisseurs of the great game.

3200 Via Centrale, Kelowna
250.765.5955 www.golfbc.com

Photographs: top and bottom right by Henebry; center right by Erica Chan; facing page top and bottom by Henebry; facing page center courtesy of The Pinnacle Course at Gallagher's Canyon

Nicklaus North Golf Course

Since the mid-1960s, championship golfer Jack Nicklaus has designed nearly 300 golf courses in more than 32 countries. Of those courses, GolfBC's Nicklaus North is one of only four to bear Jack's legendary name.

This "Signature Design" course has been the recipient of numerous awards and played host to a bevy of PGA Tour Events since its opening in 1996, but that's only a small part of its appeal. Located in the resort town of Whistler, Nicklaus North sits at the base of the breathtaking Whistler and Blackcomb mountains and along the sparkling shores of glacial-fed Green Lake. The lakeside clubhouse features a 4,000-square-foot summer patio with panoramic mountain views and overlooks Green Lake and the 16th hole.

As GolfBC's flagship property, Nicklaus North combines exceptional guest service with an environmentally conscious design that respects the area's natural habitat. Besides Jack Nicklaus, such notables as Ernie Els, Greg Norman, Fred Couples, John Daly, Vijay Singh, and Stephen Ames have all played the impeccably manicured fairways and greens of the 18-hole, par 71 championship course.

8080 Nicklaus North Boulevard, Whistler
604.938.9898 www.golfbc.com

Photographs by Henebry

Maple Ridge

Located just 45 kilometers east of Vancouver, Maple Ridge is a community with a distinct urban sensibility, a unique heritage, and spectacular natural beauty. It's the kind of place you have to see to believe, and with the new Golden Ears and Pitt River bridges, it's even easier to get there to spend a day or more participating in one of the area's many festivals or enjoying a wilderness hike.

Situated on the shores of the mighty Fraser River and nestled against the Golden Ears mountains, Maple Ridge is a mecca of adventure for the outdoor enthusiast. It is a progressive community well-known for its rolling countryside and exhilarating scenery, but is also the perfect combination of cultural hotspot and rural charm. With a population of 75,000—a number that's forecast to double within the next 20 years—Maple Ridge is clearly the place to be.

11995 Haney Place, Maple Ridge
604.467.7320 www.mapleridge.ca

Photographs: top by Oliver Rathonyi-Reusz; bottom by Jean-Pierre Robert; facing page courtesy of Maple Ridge

Arts and recreation facilities abound in Maple Ridge, creating a culturally vibrant and active community. Whether grooving to the enticing rhythms of a steel drum band at the Caribbean Street Festival, celebrating Canada's birthday with good friends, or welcoming the holiday season with the Santa Claus Parade, there is no shortage of fun to be had in Maple Ridge.

After a day of adventurous sightseeing, you're always welcome to come, see, and do more in historic downtown Maple Ridge. Explore a wide range of unique casual and gourmet restaurants offering mouthwatering fare for all tastes and budgets. Discover the latest styles and fashions at the boutique shops. Learn more about the community's history with interpretive heritage walks, or visit the studio of one of the many artists who call Maple Ridge home. Public works of art can be enjoyed at Memorial Peace Park, a relaxing green space in the heart of the community that has become the gathering place for friends new and old.

Maple Ridge is a community comfortable in the creative spotlight. The Arts Centre Theatre, known as The ACT, is the home of culture and live entertainment in Maple Ridge, showcasing both local and internationally renowned performers. In addition to world-class music and theater performances, The ACT also hosts many workshops and events throughout the year. Pottery, sculpture, painting, and drawing studios engage the public, as do ongoing exhibitions in the Maple Ridge Art Gallery.

The Haney Farmer's Market takes great pride in displaying edible works of art every Saturday from May through October. Spending a couple of relaxing hours shopping for local fresh produce, baked goods, and delicious preserves is a great way to experience the community's agricultural roots. This unique blend of small town ambience and urban sophistication is also one of the major factors in Maple Ridge being recognized as a film-friendly community. Its streets and buildings have served as backdrops depicting settings as divergent as the back streets of New York City and the highlands of Scotland.

Photographs: top and bottom courtesy of Maple Ridge; center by Devorah White; facing page left by Oliver Rathonyi-Reusz; facing page top and right courtesy of Maple Ridge

When surrounded by soaring mountains, sparkling lakes, and miles of breathtaking forested and riverfront hiking trails, it's easy to commune with nature. The options for outdoor fun in Maple Ridge are practically limitless, with mountain biking, hiking, kayaking, horseback riding, golfing, and bird watching to choose from. Alouette Lake in Golden Ears Provincial Park provides a picturesque backdrop to enjoy sailing, water-skiing, windsurfing, fishing, or a lazy afternoon on the water. While an adventurous trek to the Golden Ears summit is not for the faint of heart, hikers are rewarded with unequalled views in every direction.

Featuring over 800 kilometers of maintained trails, the majority of which are located on exceptionally scenic parkland, Maple Ridge is renowned as one of the top horseback riding areas in British Columbia. Surrounding parks provide large open spaces for sports activities, while regional and provincial parks add to the inventory of available outdoor recreation opportunities. Triathlon, running, cycling, and other individual and team sporting competitions all contribute to the vibrancy of the community and demonstrate a commitment to a healthy outdoor lifestyle throughout the year.

In 2010, the Real Estate Investment Network named Maple Ridge its number-five Top Canadian Investment City and, for the second straight year, its number-two Top BC Investment Town—calling it "the place to live for lifestyle." In addition to established industries in the agriculture and forestry sectors, growth in high tech, multimedia, education, and tourism sectors continues to generate high value jobs and fuel community development. A vibrant downtown core that offers plenty of work and play options, coupled with meticulously designed residential pockets, round out the master plan for attracting and satisfying the creative class. As testament to this dedication to excellence, Portrait Homes, a local developer and builder, has been recognized with an unprecedented total of 73 major industry provincial awards for its residential development in the Silver Valley area.

To fully appreciate Maple Ridge, visitors are encouraged to visit the many businesses and attractions that celebrate the spectacular countryside and its agricultural roots. Seasonal visits to the local blueberry and apple orchards, the Laity Pumpkin Patch, Meadows Maze, or Honeyland Canada are all considered a must for visitors to the community.

Photographs: top courtesy of Maple Ridge; middle and bottom courtesy of Portrait Homes; facing page courtesy of Kanaka Education and Environmental Partnership Society

The slogan adopted by Maple Ridge, "Deep Roots, Greater Heights," couldn't be more apt. With Kanaka Creek Falls to the east, the Golden Ears mountains to the north, the Fraser River to the south, and boundless opportunities in-between, Maple Ridge is truly a one-of-a-kind destination. Few communities so successfully combine such a strong social fabric with awe-inspiring natural beauty. Couple these amenities with a dedicated commitment to sustainability and smart growth, and even fewer communities are poised for the level of growth anticipated for the area in the coming years.

When reflecting upon the individual ingredients, it's easy to understand why Maple Ridge has become the inviting place it is today. It's been called one of British Columbia's best-kept secrets—a community of urban sophistication that continues to foster its sense of rural charm. Visitors to Maple Ridge are immediately captivated by its rare blend of an energetic urban center complemented by a variety of natural landscapes, and are amazed and inspired by its potential. Maple Ridge—come here, go far.

PACIFIC NATIONAL EXHIBITION

The Pacific National Exhibition is a Vancouver institution woven inextricably into the history of the city—a living relic and vibrant trendsetter all at once. Home to shows, exhibits, sporting events, amusement rides, concerts, cultural activities, and, of course, the annual Fair at the PNE, it encapsulates the spirit of Vancouver's heritage, achievements, and people.

Known as the Vancouver "Industrial Exhibition" when it first opened in 1910, the event began as an agricultural and industrial fair. Opening day attendance of 4,000 wowed even the most optimistic expectations, marking the fair as a stunning success right from the start and placing Vancouver solidly on the map. Over the decades, the PNE has evolved

into a perennial social gathering place reflecting the diversity of the region that provides entertainment of every sort. The site encompasses an amusement park and numerous venues that host sporting, cultural, music, and special events year-round—even serving as an Olympic site during the Vancouver 2010 Winter Olympic Games. Celebrating 100 years of fun in 2010, the PNE has become an integral part of the city.

When Vancouverites think of the Pacific National Exhibition, its 17-day fair comes first to mind for most. The Fair at the PNE is an end-of-summer tradition, a yearly extravaganza, and a world of adventure—all right in the heart of the city.

First held in 1910 and opened by Canadian Prime Minister Sir Wilfrid Laurier, the exhibition showcased the best of Vancouver and British Columbia to the rest of Canada and the world. When it began, it was the second-largest event of its kind in North America, and today it is the longest-running and best-attended—approximately one million visitors over its 17 days—annual ticketed event in BC. Many BC adults credit their first job to the fair, a tradition that holds true for today's youth as well, and citizens of all ages recall fond memories of strolling the grounds.

Over the years the PNE has grown in many ways while striving to stay true to its roots as an agricultural and industrial exhibition. In addition to amusement rides, games, and some of the most original and delicious fare around at the famous food booths, there are animal shows for livestock and pets, live performances, exhibits, showcases, contests and competitions, art displays, merchandise stalls, and much more. Even after a century of operation, the fair remains one of the most important events in a Vancouver year.

Photograph by Craig Hodge

For those who just can't wait for the 17-day late summer Fair at the PNE, there's Playland Amusement Park. This permanent attraction on the Pacific National Exhibition grounds is a 15-acre theme park open from April to October that has welcomed millions of guests of all ages since it opened in 1910. Originally the fair's games and rides area, the area was christened Happyland in 1926 and moved to its present location in 1958, reopening as Playland.

Immediately popular was the rejuvenated park's new star attraction, the Wooden Roller Coaster, which remains at the top of guests' favorite rides—and also tops the lists of the most highly regarded wooden coasters in the world. More coasters and thrill rides of all intensity levels round out the offering, while midway games allow everyone the chance to win a giant stuffed animal. A kids' area, climbing wall, mini golf course, and Haunted Mansion are some more tempting elements, and there's enough tasty treats to satisfy even the hungriest—and queasiest—stomachs. Playland is an essential component of any BC summer.

No matter the time of year, there's always something going on at the PNE. The Pacific National Exhibition grounds have evolved over the past century to include venues for music concerts, sporting events, and other performances, transforming the PNE into a hub of entertainment and family fun accessible throughout the entire year.

While the PNE grounds have always played host to various events, by the mid-20th century the economic boom and bustle was drawing more visitors all year round than ever before. In the '50s and '60s, nightlife hotspots like the Cave Supper Club drew revelers eager to view such big-time acts as Frank Sinatra and Rosemary Clooney, while the newly built, neon-emblazoned Empire Stadium hosted several legendary performances, including The Beatles and Elvis Presley, that thrilled ecstatic fans. In 1954 the British Empire and Commonwealth Games took over the stadium, allowing astonished spectators to witness both John Landy and Roger Bannister run the one-mile race in under four minutes—

an event known forever after as the "Miracle Mile." The stadium was also home to the B.C. Lions football team, with Callister Park, the Forum, and the Garden Auditorium packing in the soccer, hockey, and boxing and wrestling aficionados, respectively.

In 1968 the Pacific Coliseum opened to give the Vancouver Canucks big-league status, ready to host everything from hockey games to trade fairs and exhibitions. Today the Pacific Coliseum holds music concerts and cultural shows on a regular basis—when sports fans aren't crowding the seats.

Photographs: above by Pete Male; facing page by Craig Hodge

Official planners for the Vancouver 2010 Winter Olympic Games looked no further than the Pacific National Exhibition's very own Pacific Coliseum when deciding where to host the figure skating and short track speed skating events. It was, after all, only natural that the PNE be home to a part of an event just as monumentally significant and connected to the city's history as all the other milestones the grounds have witnessed already.

During the Games, figure skaters like Yu-Na Kim, Evan Lysacek, Johnny Weir, and Patrick Chan glided across the rink and speed skaters like Apolo Anton Ohno and François-Louis Tremblay whizzed around laps on the track—all on the same Pacific Coliseum ice. Approximately 30 changeovers took place during the games as the field of play, decked out in special blue and green Vancouver Olympic-colored padding, was adjusted to suit the sport currently taking place. The necessity of kick plates for figure skating and differing ice thickness and temperature requirements also posed a challenge—thicker, softer, 18° Celsius ice was needed for figure skating, while short track speed skating called for thinner, firmer, 16° Celsius ice. The expertise of the chief ice maker and a legion of professional ice resurface machine drivers ensured that these conditions were properly met. Such feats of engineering prove the Pacific Coliseum's versatility and ability to host a wide range of events.

With a capacity of close to 15,000 during the Olympics, the Pacific Coliseum was able to dazzle a stunning amount of fans, friends, family, and spectators who watched the athletes' performances with bated breath.

Photographs: above and facing page courtesy of Pacific National Exhibition

2010 celebrated the Pacific National Exhibition's centennial anniversary, marking 100 years since the first fair was held. The festivities culminated at the 100th summer Fair at the PNE from August 21 to September 6 with a kickoff concert featuring Bryan Adams and The Beach Boys and a special downtown PNE Parade to herald the arrival of the beloved fair.

A talent competition, kids' concerts, summer night concerts, interactive art, acrobats, a daily "100 Years of Fun" parade, displays, exhibitions, raffles, agricultural shows—as well as Playland, midway games, and delicious food as always—rounded out the unbelievable offerings as the 100th anniversary sought to top all the rest and maintain top-notch entertainment standing. Each night climaxed with the stunning finale "Kaboom!" as the pyro-musical spectacular traced the history of the PNE.

100 years strong and poised to grow even stronger, the PNE was, is, and will be the cultural touchstone of Vancouver, a gathering place for all, and a vital part of the city.

2901 East Hastings Street, Vancouver
604.253.2311 www.pne.ca

CANADA PLACE

Canada Place is a Canadian icon that embodies the lively spirit of the country. Originally built as the Canada Pavilion for the Expo '86 World's Fair, today the world-class facility serves as a hub of social and economic activity, a community gathering place, and a symbol of national pride. Canada Place's spectacular 90-foot white sails combined with promenades stretching well into the harbor resemble a ship under sail and are instantly recognizable on Vancouver's skyline.

But Canada Place is more than a landmark. It is alive with action, welcoming locals and visitors alike to step onto Canadian soil and experience a taste of Canada. Each year over three million people visit Canada Place and its stakeholders: The Pan Pacific Hotel, Vancouver Convention Centre East,

Port Metro Vancouver Cruise Ship Terminal, and World Trade Centre Office Tower. With the backdrop of the North Shore Mountains, Burrard Inlet, and Stanley Park behind each convention, scenic promenade stroll, luxury hotel escape, or cruise adventure, every activity encapsulates the essence of *the experience starts here*.

Through producing *Inspirationally Canadian* events as well as creatively fashioning a facility that represents the nation, Canada Place has emerged as a national icon—a space that instills and inspires national pride.

Photographs: above by Canada Place Corporation; facing page by Art Green

Every July 1, the award-winning Canada Day celebration rouses the hearts of over 200,000 enthusiastic guests, and each December Canada Place becomes a Christmas wonderland, all in support of charity. Throughout the year, the iconic sails are a canvas of colorful animation with the *Sails of Light* show, while Canada's Storyboard showcases stunning imagery of our country. Not to be missed is the facility's newest attraction, the Canadian Trail, which guides guests along the promenade to search out familial roots and marvel at Canada's unique towns and cities.

Standing proud, Vancouver's Canada Place continues to evolve, enlightening guests while fostering national appreciation for all the world to see.

999 Canada Place, Vancouver
604.775.7200 www.canadaplace.ca

Photographs: left by Moment Factory; top by Canada Place Corporation; bottom by Kari Medig

STEVE NASH SPORTS CLUB

Seeking a new breed of sports club? Want to work out in a green environment? Look no further than Steve Nash Sports Club, intriguingly fresh fitness facilities that promote a healthy lifestyle philosophy.

In 2007, Steve Nash—basketball point guard for the Phoenix Suns—opened the first Steve Nash Sports Club in downtown Vancouver, reflecting his passion for holistic wellbeing. One of Steve's top priorities, an integrated green design was in the blueprints from the very beginning—

each construction is LEED-approved and sets new industry standards as an example of good global citizenship.

The 38,000-square-foot state-of-the-art flagship facility also features a bamboo yoga room, massage rooms, and a juice bar. An additional 54,000-square-foot Richmond location boasts an indoor tennis complex, along with a heated indoor swimming pool and whirlpool. Green Revolution energy-generating cycling equipment, bamboo floors and

locker panels, and rubber flooring made of recycled car tires serve as further proof of the club's commitment to an eco-conscious lifestyle.

Each location doubles as a showcase for high-profile brands like Nike and lululemon athletica apparel, while offering specialty fitness classes and excellent personal training services. Innovative trainers work with patrons of all fitness levels to provide active and post-injury rehabilitation training, weight management and lifestyle modification programs, and corporate

health and wellness seminars—not to mention sport-specific conditioning regimens to meet the year-round training needs of professional hockey, soccer, baseball, football, golf, and basketball athletes.

The sports club is also a proud contributor to the Steve Nash Foundation, formed in 2001 to fund projects that provide services to children affected by poverty, illness, abuse, or neglect through grants to public service and nonprofit entities. The sports club's charitable involvement focuses,

naturally, on fitness and education initiatives, all with the aim of growing healthy kids.

President Don Harbich and founders Mark Mastrov and Leonard Schlemm, all fitness industry pioneers and luminaries, helm the sports club's operations and will lead the company to greater expansion in the future as it continues to transform the Canadian health landscape. Through its unique and admirable sustainability-friendly practices and dedication to physical wellbeing, the sports club promises to be an integral part of healthy lifestyles across Canada.

610 Granville Street, Vancouver
604.682.5213 www.stevenashsportsclub.com

10251 St. Edwards Drive, Richmond
604.273.5213 www.stevenashsportsclub.com

Photographs by Paul Joseph

THE BUTCHART GARDENS

In a time when "green" simply referred to a color and had nothing to do with sustainable practices, Jennie Butchart began an environmentally friendly plan to transform an abandoned limestone quarry into a magnificent landscape. Having already established a Japanese garden, a small rose garden near the house, and a reputation as a gardener, Jennie felt emboldened to take on the huge project of creating the sunken garden.

Encouraged by her husband and her friends, the sunken garden continued to grow and their tennis court was even transformed into the Italian garden in 1926. Her small rose garden was relocated and enlarged in 1929 and now contains some 250 varieties of roses.

Through successive generations of the Butchart family, The Gardens has retained much of its original design and continues the Edwardian tradition of seasonal changes of its outstanding floral displays. Today, owner Robin-Lee Clarke, Jennie's great-granddaughter, oversees The Gardens—now designated a National Historic Site of Canada—and ensures it retains its position as one of the world's premier floral show gardens.

Open year-round, The Butchart Gardens showcases 55 acres of flora that continuously change throughout five distinct seasons: spring, summer, autumn, Christmas, and winter-spring prelude. Special events throughout the year, such as summer Night Illuminations or the Saturday night fireworks shows, enhance the gardens within each season, too. No matter the time of year or the reason for visiting, the floral and foliage displays are sure to delight the senses.

800 Benvenuto Avenue, Brentwood Bay
250.652.5256 www.butchartgardens.com

Photographs courtesy of The Butchart Gardens Ltd.

CRAIGDARROCH CASTLE

Castles are rich with history and romance; their regal beauty inspires awe and piques curiosity. High atop two acres of rugged land with fabulous views of Victoria, Craigdarroch Castle is the epitome of Victorian wealth and grandeur. Commissioned and built between 1887 and 1890 for Robert Dunsmuir—a Scottish immigrant who made his fortune from Vancouver Island coal—the carefully restored, legendary mansion with formal gardens marks an era of industrialization and is the architectural legacy of one of the most prominent families in Western Canada.

Stepping into the circular carriage entrance for your self-guided tour is the beginning of a rare and magical experience. The immense fortune of the Dunsmuirs is reflected in the four floors of exquisite stained glass windows, intricate woodwork, and Victorian furnishings filling 39 rooms. Visitors are invited to make the winding climb up 87 stairs to the castle tower for breathtaking vistas of Victoria, the Strait of Juan de Fuca, and the Olympic Mountains. Beyond daily walking tours, private events are commonplace, as the 20,000-square-foot estate was originally intended for lavish entertaining, and the castle can be reserved for special gatherings of up to 200 guests. Owned and operated by the Craigdarroch Castle Historical Museum Society, a charitable organization, Victoria's legendary landmark offers a memorable glimpse into the splendor of a Victorian lifestyle.

1050 Joan Crescent, Victoria
250.592.5323 www.thecastle.ca

Photographs courtesy of Craigdarroch Castle Historical Society

Nanaimo

If Nanaimo could only boast about the fact that it has one of the longest shorelines in Canada, visitors would still have a plethora of activities to keep them busy. With such mild weather year-round, pastimes like snorkeling with seals in an undersea grotto, sea kayaking in the bay, sunbathing on the numerous beaches, and catching crab off a downtown pier are only a few of the intriguing things to do in the "Harbour City."

But Nanaimo offers much more than just an exquisite shoreline. In fact, the city and surrounding area have just about everything a person could want. There's fine food, including a wide array of ethnic cuisines and Canada's only floating pub. There's high adventure, with an aerial adventure park complete with bungee jumping, zip lines, and a treetop obstacle course. And there's a thriving arts scene, with galleries, museums, theater, the symphony, and a 250-seat performing arts center.

And after all of that, if visitors still desire something else to tickle their fancy, Nanaimo offers some of the funkiest festivals in the province, including the famous World Championship Bathtub Race. Nature lovers can take part in the outdoors with more than 200 parks and scores of hiking and biking trails—not to mention Newcastle Island Marine Provincial Park, the Harbourfront Walkway, and Mount Benson in the city's backyard. The list could go on and on, but one thing's for certain: the beautiful shore is just the beginning for all of the activities available in Nanaimo.

Nanaimo
800.663.7337 www.tourismnanaimo.com

Photographs courtesy of the City of Nanaimo

OLE'S HAKAI PASS

Imagine landing a 20-pound acrobatic coho or trophy chinook salmon, a huge halibut, a ling or a snapper! It's a fisherman's dream, but can be your reality at Ole's. The pristine Central West Coast offers some of the most envied waters for sport fishing the world over. That's why angling adventures at Ole's Hakai Pass fly-in lodge are unsurpassed. Located in Hakai Luxvbalis Conservancy Area, the largest protected marine park on British Columbia's coast, exciting fishing opportunities abound in the sheltered waters. From Vancouver, a breathtaking two-hour flight concludes with the float plane landing at the Hakai Pass dock on the remote Central Coast. Ole's comfortable, relaxing floating lodge opens its doors from July to early September. Many guests return annually for repeat trips with fellow fishermen, business associates, friends, and family, eager to create lively fish tales for posterity.

This unspoiled area was discovered by the Olsen logging family back in the 1950s, leading to Ole's founding in 1982 by Irv and Joanne Olsen. An ideal location for a fishing lodge, Ole's is situated in a protected bay within minutes of the best fishing grounds. This secluded territory is home to fascinating wildlife and sea mammals including humpback whales, dolphins, sea lions, bald eagles, and seals; Ole's enthusiastically supports local hatcheries and coastal communities to help preserve nature's gifts. These nutrient-rich waters entice migrating chinook and voracious coho salmon, bottom-loving halibut, yellow-eye rockfish, and ling cod. Ole's has the best fishing variety and opportunities in the Pacific Northwest, attracting novice to expert anglers. Lodge guests also enjoy après fishing activities, including the outdoor hot tub with an awesome 360-degree view, sea kayaking, a daily menu of gourmet comfort food with a well-stocked bar, and comfortable private rooms. Above all, Ole's laid-back atmosphere of camaraderie fosters lasting friendships. For the experience of a lifetime, Ole's is your destination. Go ahead, book your trip. Then post that happy sign on your door quoting Satchmo's whistle-worthy tune: "Gone fishin'..."

PO Box 753, Campbell River
250.287.8303 www.ole.ca

Photographs: top left by Andrew Moncrief; bottom left by Blake McBurney; all others by Ernie Daley

ROYAL LONDON WAX MUSEUM

History. Celebrity. Pop culture. Inspiration springs from people born before us and those who live among us. Founded in 1961, Royal London Wax Museum is one of the finest collections of wax sculpture in North America. It pays homage to the past and present: European royalty, pivotal historical figures, and illustrious people whom we know and love. The art of wax modeling has roots to ancient Egypt, early Rome, and the Middle Ages, with the French Revolution, the guillotine, and Marie Grosholtz (later Tussaud) laying the foundation for modern-day wax museums. Now, as then, exquisite realistic wax sculptures are created to capture famous personages for all to enjoy, much to the delight of admirers of all ages.

Madame Tussaud's Wax Museum in London was aptly described by one French ambassador: "A day in Tussaud's is worth a year at Oxford; it fixes history as no tutor could." This rich educational benefit is also true of Victoria's Royal London Wax Museum, which follows in the tradition of Old World establishments. The gallery features more than 300 wax likenesses of contemporary and historic figures—from royals, religious icons, and political figures, to sports greats, Hollywood stars, inventors, musicians, literary geniuses, and infamous characters. Beautiful replicas of the Crown Jewels of England are also proudly on display. Multimedia presentations further illuminate guests with interesting facts about the museum's displays while bringing a little bit of old England to the heart of Victoria.

Victoria, British Columbia
250.388.4461 www.waxmuseum.bc.ca

Photographs courtesy of Royal London Wax Museum

BC Place

A new skyline. A new architectural icon. The largest cable-supported retractable roof in the world. Sound checks are starting. Crowds are cheering. BC Place is a world-class events venue that stays in your mind from the moment you enter until long after the lights dim and the excitement comes to a close. The iconic stadium has been an emblem of British Columbia for more than 25 years. Built in 1983, over 27 million people have passed through its doors to attend everything from trade and consumer shows to sporting events, performances, and grand-scale gatherings including the awe-inspiring opening and closing ceremonies of the Vancouver 2010 Olympic Winter Games. Whether hosting B.C. Lions football games, Whitecaps FC soccer matches, epic concerts, or spectacular corporate events of all kinds, BC Place has it all.

BC Place offers 55,000 seats at capacity with 250,000 square feet of exhibit space. Originally covered by a unique air-supported roof, the stadium is now topped off with an innovative, automated retractable roof. The "blue-sky" roof was designed to extend the stadium's versatility for year-round use and allows BC Place to offer spectacular open-air events under starlight and warm sunshine. BC Place may very well be the true centerpiece of Vancouver; from the air it appears at the heart and center of one of the most vibrant cities of Western Canada. Attracting local Canadians and international visitors alike, BC Place has made its mark and continues to evolve. As part of the revitalization of False Creek, the stadium is steadily contributing to a new era of job creation, adding substantial environmental and economic benefits to the province. Whether you're perched in a private suite, cushy club seat, or chair dozens of rows up in a packed stadium, any BC Place event is an experience you'll remember for years to come.

777 Pacific Boulevard, Vancouver
604.669.2300 www.bcplace.com

Photographs: Above and facing page top center and bottom right by Hubert King; facing page top left, top right, and center by Ema Peter; facing page bottom left courtesy of BC Place

BC SPORTFISHING GROUP

Nestled among stunning mountains and interspersed with numerous waterways, Harrison Hot Springs is a sport fisher's paradise. Dynamic lakes and rivers filled with incredible returns of wild salmon, steelhead trout, and white sturgeon, along with several successful fish hatcheries, have made fishing in this region something anglers far and wide come to experience.

Tony Nootebos, who has been fishing local rivers, lakes, and streams since he was four years old, knows the spectacular valley inside and out; his father cultivated in him a love for fishing and a respect for nature. In an effort to showcase his native area and help others see its beauty, Tony now leads BC Sportfishing Group, which he helped found in 1997. Along with 22 fully insured and licensed fishing guides, he and his team provide world-class sport fishing experiences while respecting the sustainability of their familiar local resources.

With a goal to deliver the finest outdoor experience possible, Tony and his guides take guests on unforgettable adventures using their fleet of 22 boats and high-quality equipment. Each fishing trip is also a tutorial during which the well-educated guides enjoy passing on their knowledge of sport fishing and the resources they use every day. Whether the ideal experience includes a one-day sturgeon trip or a multi-day sport fishing holiday, a search for salmon or a quest for trout, a walk-and-wade or boat-fishing trip, the guides at BC Sportfishing Group promise you the guided sport fishing holiday of a lifetime.

100 Esplanade, Harrison Hot Springs
877.796.3345 www.bcsportfishinggroup.com

Photographs by Anthony R. Nootebos

Big Bus

Visitors to Vancouver are now going topless throughout the city—by riding on the city's only open-top retro single-level and vintage double-decker buses, that is. Begun in 2004 as a nod to London's original hop-on, hop-off tour buses, Big Bus provides an exciting, open-air way to see the city. And now, a recent partnership with Big Bus of Victoria allows visitors to receive the same experience in two cities.

Centered in historic Gastown, the Vancouver buses run year-round and offer 22 stops that cover sights from the sandy beaches of English Bay to the snow-capped mountains nestled against the shore. With each ticket providing two days of service within a two-week period, Big Bus leaves travelers plenty of time to stop off at their favorite sites.

Not only do your eyes get a treat with the tour but your ears and taste buds can too. Professionally recorded commentary in more than seven languages provides an entertaining tour. Big Bus' welcome center is the perfect spot for a mid-afternoon snack. Delicious fudge and gelato are made in-house and are even included in the price of some tickets. Regardless of which senses are used, sit on the top deck of the bus to enjoy an exhilarating ride.

317 Water Street, Vancouver
877.299.0701 www.bigbus.ca

Photographs courtesy of Jewdin Media, Inc.

CAPILANO SUSPENSION BRIDGE

What do you do if the best fishing access to the river you live on is across a 450-foot gorge? If you're founder George Grant Mackay, you build a suspension bridge 230 feet above the floor of Capilano Canyon and march over Capilano River whenever you please.

Vancouver's oldest attraction, Capilano Suspension Bridge, was built in 1889 with hemp rope and cedar planks, a far cry from the bridge as it is today made of steel cables capable of supporting the weight of two 747 jets. Surrounded by a 28-acre natural park dense with towering evergreens, steep cliffs, and lush terrain, the bridge offers an array of cultural, historical, and environmental exhibits for those with a zest for regional knowledge.

The Capilano experience has expanded to offer more enriching experiences to British Columbia sightseers thanks to native Vancouverite and Canadian tourism leader Nancy Stibbard, who acquired the landmark in 1983 and has since brought it fully to life. Under her enthusiastic guidance, Capilano has garnered numerous awards while enjoying record-breaking visitor numbers. Great fun for outdoor enthusiasts and thrill-seekers, guests can take in an eco-friendly Treetops Adventure with an owl's eye view from a uniquely engineered forest walkway made up of seven suspension bridges. And at the Little Big House, visitors can share in the arts, storytelling, and culture of native First Nations people. A true British Columbia wonder, the woodland attraction promises active outdoor excitement for everyone—just 10 minutes from downtown Vancouver.

3735 Capilano Road, North Vancouver
604.985.7474 www.capbridge.com

Photographs by Capilano Group of Companies

CASCADES CASINO AND COAST HOTEL & CONVENTION CENTRE

Looking for an inviting place to relax and have a little fun in Langley? Look no further than Cascades Casino, where the staff and employees have perfected fun. They know how to make guests feel welcome, bring out a smile, and exceed every expectation.

Located in downtown Langley—an excellent big-city detour where historic sites abound and activities will satisfy even the most finicky traveler—Cascades Casino provides a variety of entertainment in one stop. As the largest casino in the Fraser Valley, with more than 80,000 square feet of gaming space, all of the favorite games are ready to be played. Need a more passive pursuit? Be wowed in the 420-seat Summit Theatre that showcases year-round performances with concerts, comedy, and private celebrations, or stay in the middle of the action at the Glacier Lounge, which offers ongoing sports viewing on the big screen as well as live entertainment. At the end of the day, two dining options—The Pinnacle Grille and Lobby Café—will satisfy those cravings. Whether it's to stay and play or meet and greet, the adjacent Coast Hotel & Convention Centre offers 77 guestrooms and 25,000 square feet of convention space—and the means to get comfortable and relax in a casual environment designed just for you.

20393 Fraser Highway, Langley
604.530.2211 www.cascadescasino.ca

Photographs courtesy of Cascades Casino and Coast Hotel & Convention Centre

CITY OF PITT MEADOWS

In a unique blend of urban appeal and rural charm, Pitt Meadows is a quaint city that lies at the intersection of the metropolitan and agricultural centers of the region. With its compact, pedestrian-friendly downtown area and unparalleled scenic surroundings, Pitt Meadows has become the natural place to live, work, play, and invest.

Traveling there could not be easier. In addition to the city's proximity to Vancouver and its various modes of transportation, Pitt Meadows Regional Airport provides a nice alternative with three runways, a float plane launch and dock, and aviation hangar sites.

Once in the community, a plethora of experiences await you. Book your tee time at Pitt Meadows Golf Club and enjoy perfectly manicured lawns and a picturesque backdrop, or experience the thrill of a lifetime with Pacific Skydivers on a flight into the big blue sky followed by an exhilarating freefall and parachute back down to the ground.

The nearby Pitt Lake, the largest tidal lake in North America and the rumored location of Slumach's lost gold mine, is just the beginning of the outstanding adventures available. Road cycling, exploring Scenic Highway 7, picnicking in a park, or taking the Circle Farm Tour are just a few more ideas of what's possible in a visit to Pitt Meadows. The only difficult part? Deciding what to do first!

Pitt Meadows
604.465.5454 www.pittmeadows.bc.ca

Photographs: top left courtesy of Pitt Meadows Airport; top right by Guy Bryck for Pacific Skydivers; bottom left courtesy of City of Pitt Meadows; bottom right courtesy of Pitt Meadows Golf Club

COOPER BOATING

Located on historic Granville Island, just a few minutes' sail from English Bay, Cooper Boating is Canada's largest charter agency and recreational boating school. It maintains a fleet of 65 spectacular yachts with a seasoned crew of instructors and staff, all intent on helping guests enjoy the beauty of the water and the surrounding landscape.

The Jib Set Sailing Club, a cooperative, offers creative access to boats. Participants share boats—a dozen per vessel—and pay a monthly fee that allows them to be on the water as much as they'd like. Each boat flies the trademark red jib sail.

Originally founded by Forbes Cooper, an icon of the boating industry in Vancouver, the company was purchased by owner Colin Jackson's father

in 1988, and taken over by Colin in 1996. It is one of the few remaining boating businesses that line Mast Tower Road, which derived its name from the masts built and stepped at the end of the street.

The crew also operates out of the breathtaking Port Sidney marina on Vancouver Island and seasonally out of Powell River, just south of idyllic Desolation Sound.

1815 Mast Tower Road, Vancouver
604.687.4110 www.cooperboating.com

Photographs by www.insightphotography.com

DR. SUN YAT-SEN CLASSICAL CHINESE GARDEN

During China's Ming dynasty, believed to be the apex of Chinese culture, scholars enjoyed elite status and private gardens. How lucky, then, that citizens and visitors to Vancouver have access to their very own Ming scholar garden incarnation in the form of the Dr. Sun Yat-Sen Classical Chinese Garden.

As the first Chinese garden to be built outside of China, it opened on April 24, 1986, in time for Expo '86. Just as Dr. Sun Yat-Sen, the garden's namesake and an enduring social icon considered the father of modern China, changed the face of China by serving as a bridge to Western ideas, so too does the garden itself bridge cultures. Thanks to its role as an embodiment of classical China and the centerpiece of Chinatown, it simultaneously supplies and sustains Eastern cultures in a Western land—linking up disparate Vancouver communities.

Joe Wai, the Chinese Garden's architect, and Don Vaughan, the landscape architect, sought to offer an example of Chinese culture that blended with its surroundings and incorporated aspects of both. Funded by both Chinese and Canadian sources, it was built by 53 master craftsmen from China, alongside Canadian counterparts, utilizing traditional Chinese building methods—no glue, nails, or screws. Four elements balance and coalesce in Chinese gardens—water, rock, plants, and architecture—and Wai and Vaughan's design plans duly uphold this principle. Rocks and plants were imported from China, but local botany flourishes as well—after all, its mandate is to bridge cultures.

Under the executive direction of Kathy Gibler, the Chinese Garden offers tours and programs like concert nights to connect to the community regularly. For aesthetes, historians, botanists, or anyone who simply enjoys peaceful places, this will prove a delightful stroll through a fascinating urban haven.

578 Carrall Street, Vancouver
604.662.3207 www.vancouverchinesegarden.com

Photographs by Lauchlin McKenzie

DEELEY MOTORCYCLE EXHIBITION

Trev Deeley, a BC motorcycling legend, collected motorcycles from the 1950s until his death in 2002. During this time he amassed a collection of over 250 motorcycles, representing over 50 brands and valued at more than $3 million. The scope of such an assortment, currently one of the largest private motorcycle collections in Canada, offers such a wide range of interest that it's sure to entertain and intrigue novices and experts alike.

Don James and Malcolm Hunter of Deeley Harley-Davidson Canada own and operate Deeley Motorcycle Exhibition, which promotes the sport and art of motorcycling. The collection is rotated through the exhibition hall in themed exhibits of approximately 70 machines at a time. All makes and models are showcased in an approachable and relaxed environment—none of the bikes are roped off. A huge three-dimensional map of BC and Washington State projects ride routes, and associated computer terminals at the map allow visitors to examine the routes in greater detail and use them to plan a trip by printing out a personal map. There's even a vintage bike and sidecar with a backdrop for photo opportunities.

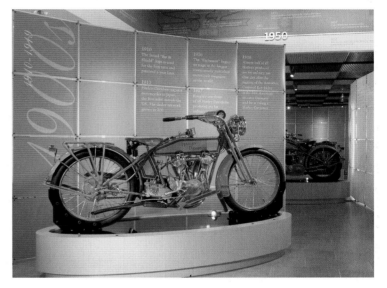

The ever-growing collection boasts rare finds ranging from an 1894 Hildebrandt Wolf-Mueller—the first two-wheeled vehicle to be registered as a motorcycle—to a 1906 Indian "Camelback" and a mint 2009 MV Agusta #32/100, a recent acquisition. How best to sum up the exhibition staff's attitude? As Trev Deeley once said, "It doesn't matter what you ride, just as long as you ride."

1875 Boundary Road, Vancouver
604.293.2221 www.deeleymotorcycleexhibition.ca

Photographs by Perry Danforth

FORT LANGLEY NATIONAL HISTORIC SITE

The gold rush era of the Fraser River region gave rise to Fort Langley as the birthplace of the colony of British Columbia. It was proclaimed a Crown Colony in 1858 by James Douglas to avoid annexation by the U.S. and protect Canada's valuable discovery. But it was in 1827 that the Hudson's Bay Company built Fort Langley on the mighty river as a fur trading post for Aboriginal peoples. Not only were furs shipped to Europe via Cape Horn, produce was traded to the Russians in Alaska, local cranberries found their way to California, and wild salmon catches were sent as far away as Hawaii.

Fort Langley is one of Parks Canada's national treasures. Today, one original building blends with newer constructions on the historic trading site where visitors can watch fascinating demonstrations by costumed interpreters donning period clothing for an authentic experience. Fort Langley National Historic Site gives many glimpses into the past: you can observe the Old World art of barrel-making, see molten iron being hand-forged as you hear the ringing of the anvil in the blacksmith shop, or try your hand panning for gold nuggets in streaming waters. Interactive exhibits, activities, and storytelling by lively performers present a fun educational experience while expressing the heart and soul of Canadians, their native culture and pioneering spirit. Since 1931, families and travelers have been inspired by the marriage of commerce and culture at historic Fort Langley, a meaningful place that has forever changed the map of Canada. Plan to learn a lot and linger a while at Fort Langley, open year-round, then take a leisurely stroll in its neighboring village brimming with artists' studios, bookstores, specialty boutiques, and antiques shops, all under tree-lined streets amid a charming, country atmosphere.

23433 Mavis Avenue, Fort Langley
604.513.4777 www.pc.gc.ca/fortlangley

Photographs courtesy of Parks Canada (Michael Boland)

FORT RODD HILL AND FISGARD LIGHTHOUSE NATIONAL HISTORIC SITES

The majestic Fisgard Lighthouse, once a call home for sailors, now beckons to the more than 40,000 tourists who visit the lighthouse and adjacent Fort Rodd Hill each year. Spanning more than 44 acres, these national historic sites are beacons of opportunity to discovering British Columbia's natural and cultural history. Fisgard Lighthouse was built in 1860 as the first permanent lighthouse on Canada's West Coast, safely ushering mariners home to Victoria and Esquimalt. Not only the oldest lighthouse on the West Coast, it is one of the oldest homes in Victoria. Learn about the architecture and technology behind mid-Victorian brick lighthouses and further explore what life was like back then. Step inside the charming keeper's house and enjoy engaging exhibits with a welcoming staff to guide you.

Further explorations of the grounds reveal a fort ripe for investigation by curious travelers. Built in the late 1890s, Fort Rodd Hill's gun batteries protected the busy port of Victoria and the naval base at Esquimalt Harbour. Throughout two world wars, its secret underground magazines, command posts, guardhouses, barracks, and searchlights were stalwart sentinels in the defense of Canada and the British Empire. During World War II, soldiers kept close watch for maritime traffic entering Juan de Fuca Strait that might threaten the commercial and shipbuilding ports of Victoria and Vancouver. The original fort was built for defense, but now it's a haven for black-tailed deer, river otters, and harbor seals, and a place where native eagles, herons, ducks, and songbirds delight avid birders. Bring your camera and wander through this legendary site at your own pace. See majestic ships from slender sloops to cargo carriers gliding down the channel. Plan to picnic under mighty Garry oak trees or relax on the breezy seashore.

603 Fort Rodd Hill Road, Victoria
250.478.5849 www.pc.gc.ca/fisgardlighthouse

Photographs courtesy of Parks Canada

GOLF BRITISH COLUMBIA

Golf in British Columbia has a rich and storied history. Oceanside, parkland, desert, forest, and mountain courses have offered tremendous variety and memorable experiences since before the turn of the 19th century.

The origins of the British Columbia Golf Association can be dated to 1893 when a mandate to hold a provincial championship was created. Now, more than 117 years later, the association is the governing body for golf in the province and administers a membership that includes more than 62,000 individual golfers at more than 300 member clubs and facilities.

In 1894, the first amateur golfing championship in BC was held at the Victoria Golf Club. The winner was awarded a trophy donated by Hewitt Bostock, the Lt. Governor of the province. The trophy, known as the Bostock Cup, is still awarded today and is believed to be the oldest trophy, continuously competed for in North America.

Golf served as one of the first sports that encouraged the participation of women. The resulting popularity brought about the first ladies' amateur championship, also held in Victoria, in 1895. In 1905, Alfred C. Flumerfelt, a member of the Victoria Golf Club, donated a cup for the BC ladies' championship. The Flumerfelt Cup continues to be raised by the BC amateur women's champion and is the oldest women's trophy still played for in North America.

As the consumer-facing brand for the BC Golf Association, Golf British Columbia proudly represents the sport of golf throughout the province. The association enthusiastically advocates on behalf of the sport and supports the history of the game in British Columbia.

2110-13700 Mayfield Place, Richmond
604.279.2580 www.golfbritishcolumbia.ca

Photographs: top and center by Amanda Malone; bottom by Barrie McWha

GOLDEN EAGLE GOLF CLUB

Not many golf courses can boast natural beauty both throughout the links and surrounding them, but that's what you'll find at Golden Eagle Golf Club—36 championship holes bordered on all sides by breathtaking scenery.

Golden Eagle's North course opened in 1994, with the South following a year later. Since then, both 18-hole courses have provided scores of locals and visitors with fair tests to any skill level, welcoming staff, and stunning scenery. Located 45 minutes outside Vancouver and only seven mintues from the new Golden Ears Bridge, Golden Eagle is nestled at the foot of the majestic snow-capped Thompson Mountains. The signature third hole on the South course runs right alongside the mountain for most of its 406 yards, and the North course's signature 15th hole also features a stunning mountain landscape—not to mention a large sand trap and a carry over water to an undulating green.

When it's time to pack up the clubs and unwind, the club's award-winning patio supplies a hard-to-beat spot for watching the sunset while enjoying food and drink from the Eagle's Nest Bar & Grill. While traversing the course or relaxing on the patio, you might catch a glimpse of nearby wandering deer, Sandhill cranes, or even a golden eagle or two. Now that's definitely nature.

21770 Ladner Road, Pitt Meadows
604.460.1111 www.goldeneaglegolfclub.com

Photographs by Lorae Brickwood

GOLF HOLIDAYS WEST

If your ideal vacation involves strolling a well-manicured lawn with the goal of tapping a small white sphere into a tiny hole, then Golf Holidays West should be your new best friend. Founded out of the Webb family's love for and appreciation of the sport, the company focuses on orchestrating the best golf experience in settings worldwide.

A location in British Columbia obviously affords Jeff and Anne, partners in life as well as in business, insider knowledge of the local courses. Yet they also bring exceptional expertise about the best greens around the globe, both from research as well as personal experiences from their far-reaching travels. From breathtaking views on Maui to variety in Asia, Golf Holidays West has a package ready to suit individual needs—and if one doesn't exist, they'll build a custom getaway experience. With more than three decades in the industry, Jeff and Anne have established relationships throughout the golf world, which comes in handy for those who desire special tickets for the Masters or tee times at St. Andrews.

108-216 East 6th Street, North Vancouver
604.669.1434 www.golfholidayswest.com

Photographs courtesy of Golf Holidays West

GULF OF GEORGIA CANNERY NATIONAL HISTORIC SITE

Throughout its history, West Coast fishing has helped fuel the economy and enrich the social fabric of British Columbia. This vibrant heritage is justly celebrated in Steveston Village, which was, and remains, an important center of the West Coast fishing industry. One of the province's few historically intact canneries, the Gulf of Georgia Cannery National Historic Site commemorates the development of the industry from the 1870s to the present.

Situated atop wooden pilings over the mighty Fraser River, the cannery's wooden building features 55,000 square feet of sounds, images, and artifacts that detail its history since 1894. Inside the Boiler House Theatre—a one-of-a-kind space that includes three huge boilers that originally generated steam power for the cannery's machinery—the award-winning film "Journey Through Time" depicts happenings in the fishing industry. Numerous other exhibits bring to life the machines that once churned out millions of cans of salmon. A walk through its exhibits brings visitors face to face with the Chinese, Japanese, First Nations, and European fishermen and plant workers who toiled long hours to keep up with the mountain of sockeye that were once processed there.

After strolling through the museum, touring with a guide, and participating in various activities—such as punching a time card and learning from hands-on exhibits—things like seining, gillnetting, trolling, longlining, and trawling will all make sense. The workers' experiences will not be forgotten, and a significant part of British Columbia's history will continue to live on in every visitor.

12138 4th Avenue, Richmond
604.664.9009 www.gulfofgeorgiacannery.com

Photographs by Ken Mayer

KRAUSE BERRY FARMS

Alf Krause began growing strawberries and raspberries back in 1974. The endeavor has expanded ever since, and today Krause Berry Farms is a successful and diverse family business. The 165-acre farm is known for its "Good Farming Practices," meaning it employs sustainable crop rotation, eco-friendly fertilization, and other techniques that focus on the land's long-term future. Loyal patrons love knowing where, how, and by whom their food is grown.

From June to October, thousands of folks eager for fresh strawberries, raspberries, blueberries, and blackberries descend upon Krause Berry Farms, where 40 "U-Pick" acres await. Whether you want a basket of berries for dessert or pounds for preserves, you'll feel the health benefits and taste the freshness with every bite.

Over the years, Krause Berry Farms has grown into one of the most popular and well-respected examples of agri-tourism in British Columbia. In addition to the bountiful berry fields, the farm kitchen is renowned for its famous berry custard pies, trademark shortcakes, and berry ice cream. It's fascinating to watch the bakers through the panoramic viewing windows as they prepare their sweet and savory treats from scratch daily. Take in the beauty of the farm as you relax on the wraparound porch and treat yourself to a refreshing old-fashioned berry milkshake and homegrown corn pizza. A selection of farm vegetables and products are available for purchase by guests, including homemade jams, jellies, syrups, and gourmet preserves made with berries and vegetables grown right on the farm.

Alf and his wife Sandee transform the farm into a Christmas wonderland each November and December. Guests eagerly purchase fresh Christmas baking for their holiday gatherings while enjoying horse-drawn carriage rides, wreath and bread making workshops, as well as visits from Santa.

Krause Berry Farms is the first job for many of the community's teens. As parents of six children themselves, Alf and Sandee take this responsibility seriously, preparing more than just the land for a bright future.

6179 248th Street, Langley
604.856.5757 www.krauseberryfarms.com

Photographs courtesy of Krause Berry Farms

LimoJet Gold

Limousines. The word conjures notions of fame and fortune, or the rare glitzy special event worth the splurge—in short, too fancy for everyday life. But that's not so at LimoJet Gold, a limousine transportation service that aims to provide affordable yet high-end travel assistance to the average visitor without the celebrity cost. With rates that remain constant year-round—without sacrificing safety or reliability—a luxury limousine to chauffeur you around the Vancouver area is more accessible than you dreamed.

CEO Herb Dhaliwal and vice president Mike Olak both emigrated to Canada from India seeking a better life—and have since gained 60 combined years of business experience. Prioritizing health and family, both executives honor their roots despite their professional success, and it's that down-to-earth quality that makes the limousine company so feasible for any income level.

LimoJet seeks to be more than just a way to get people from Point A to Point B—it ensures that drivers serve as courteous and knowledgeable ambassadors to the city, presenting visitors with veritable urban tours. This guarantees that travelers leave happy and with that positive, lasting impression so crucial to word of mouth recommendations. Operating out of Richmond, the company had served as Vancouver International Airport's sole official limousine transportation provider for a period of over 20 years.

A fleet of sleek Lincoln vehicles in a variety of sizes, types, and colors services both local and international clientele for all kinds of purposes—whether bridal or formal parties, professionals or executives, celebrities or VIPs, or terminally ill children for charity, all receive the gold standard that LimoJet has made its hallmark.

Suite 140-4651 Shell Road, Richmond
604.273.1331 www.limojetgold.com

Photographs by Philipe Martin-Morice; PMM Photography

MINTER GARDENS

On Christmas Day 1977, Brian and Faye Minter, owners of the Country Garden Store in Chilliwack, stumbled upon a unique landscape nestled against 7,000-foot Mt. Cheam. Immediately, they recognized the beauty and potential of the area and began to put their dreams into action. Just a few years later, the couple opened the 32-acre, world-famous Minter Gardens as a place to share their passions with the community.

Today the display garden is a stunning array of nature showcased in 12 themed areas. Still owned and operated by the Minters, their two daughters Lisa and Erin and son-in-law Glen, the gardens offer sights, sounds, and aromas that will dazzle the senses. More than 100,000 tulips portray majestic color in the spring, along with other delightful spring bulbs. Brilliant annual color and vibrant roses are in bloom throughout the summer and peak during July and August. Throughout the growing season, guests mingle amidst babbling brooks and tumbling waterfalls, relax in the restaurant or café, and feel the mist of the stunning 'Spirit of the Falls' waterwall.

The Minters' passion for the gardens and their staff's dedication has transformed this unique area of land into a gorgeous destination and a gateway to the mountains for all to enjoy.

52892 Bunker Road, Rosedale
888.646.8377 www.mintergardens.com

Photographs by Adam Gibbs

MORGAN CREEK GOLF COURSE

Perfectly mirroring the high quality of the stunning scenery and manicured greens, Morgan Creek Golf Course enables members and visitors to revel in the luxurious atmosphere and service that is well known in the community. Director of Golf Wayne Vollmer ensures that guests feel like esteemed club members for the day, believing every golfer's visit should be a memorable experience.

Situated among mildly rolling hills with the North Shore Mountains as the background, Morgan Creek was created by *Golf Digest* award-winning Canadian designer Thomas McBroom in 1995 as a residential golf community that heartily welcomes all players.

Situated on 160 acres including nearly 90 acres of natural landscape, the course boasts a terrific attention to detail. Throughout the undulating 18 holes, the unique line of play is challenging yet fair to all levels, from the novice to the experienced professional. In addition, a beautiful clubhouse, banquet facility, wedding gardens, and an upscale casual restaurant with wine bar add to the amenities that led to the PGA of BC's selection of Morgan Creek as Golf Facility of the Year.

3500 Morgan Creek Way, Surrey
604.531.4653 www.morgancreekgolf.com

Photographs by John Johnston

PEACE PORTAL GOLF CLUB

Samuel Hill, a visionary who excelled in law, railway management, and construction, first stumbled upon the idea of a golf club in 1921. He was commemorating 100 years of peace between Canada and the United States through the opening of the International Peace Arch on the border between what is now Surrey, British Columbia, and Blaine, Washington. With Prohibition in full swing in the States, Sam became inspired to build a golf club and resort near the border for his forcibly "dry" American friends.

By 1927, Semiahmoo Club opened with delicious cuisine and, of course, liquor. The club was an immediate hit; yet throughout construction of the golf course, the media often called his project "ridiculous." But beginning in 1929 when the first nine holes opened and continuing after all 18 holes at Peace Portal Golf Club officially opened in 1932, the course has been a success.

Today the 132-acre course is similar to its grand beginnings, with just a few minor renovations. The natural surroundings have matured to a beautiful park-like setting with nary a building in sight. With variety found at each hole, like the 461-yard 5th hole or the 17th with the lake on the left and the river on the right, the experience is challenging and intriguing.

16900 4th Avenue, Surrey
604.538.4818 www.peaceportalgolf.com

Photographs by Bruce Garton

RICHMOND OLYMPIC OVAL

Located minutes from Vancouver International Airport, the Richmond Olympic Oval is a breathtaking venue along the banks of the Fraser River and a hallmark of public accessibility, environmental sustainability, and world-class sportsmanship. Built by the City of Richmond and operated by the Richmond Oval Corporation, the venue was completed well in advance of the Vancouver 2010 Winter Olympic Games, officially opening to the public in December of 2008.

Honored with several awards including the Institution of Structural Engineers 2009 Award for Sports or Leisure Structures, the building has spacious, modern interiors featuring wood floors, natural light, and a broad public art program incorporated into the Oval itself and its immediate surroundings.

During the 2010 Winter Olympic Games, the Oval seated 8,000 for 12 long-track speed skating events that saw 36 medals awarded. Today it serves as the centerpiece of an active urban waterfront neighborhood. An international center of excellence for sports, health, and wellness, the Oval offers a complete range of sports medicine and wellness services, a 23,000-square-foot fitness center, and multi-functional space on the activity level, which accommodates ice, track, and court users. In addition, the Oval provides a state-of-the-art indoor paddling tank and studio space for group fitness, yoga, cycling, and rowing.

This renowned facility offers an inspiring environment for all skill levels—from fitness rookies to sports superstars—to progress toward their own personal podiums.

6111 River Road, Richmond
778.296.1400 www.richmondoval.ca

Photographs: top right by VANOC; center right by Jeff Vinnick; bottom right by British Columbia Forestry Innovation Investment (BCFII); facing page by Ted Huang

ROCKY MOUNTAINEER

Consistently recognized as one of the greatest rail journeys in the world, Rocky Mountaineer offers luxurious, breathtaking train experiences through Canada's West and the Canadian Rockies. For 20 years, the BC-based organization has hosted more than a million international travelers, catering to those with a passion for historical adventure, an appreciation for natural wonders, or a desire to see world-class destinations.

Travelers can choose from four spectacular rail routes and over 45 vacation packages that showcase the diverse beauty of the Western Canadian provinces of BC and Alberta, including a three-hour trip between Vancouver and Whistler or an eight-day tour which highlights the best of the Canadian Rockies. Rocky Mountaineer's signature two-day, all-daylight train excursions feature sights such as Hell's Gate, an extinct volcano, the Spiral Tunnels, the Continental Divide, rolling ranchlands, Banff National Park, and Pyramid Falls—not to mention plenty of wildlife in their natural habitat. All of this is experienced in the comfort of a well-appointed railcar or bi-level dome coach featuring an outdoor vestibule, dining car, and front-row views of the passing landscape.

With each journey, guests experience world-renowned service and informative, entertaining commentary from gracious onboard attendants. Travelers also dine on three-course, à la carte meals created using fresh ingredients indigenous to BC and Alberta by a team of gourmet chefs when traveling in GoldLeaf Service. With a choice of upscale GoldLeaf Service or classic RedLeaf Service, guests enjoy the spectacular scenery of Western Canada while having the best travel experience of their lives.

Vancouver
604.606.7245 www.rockymountaineer.com

Photographs: top and bottom courtesy of Robert G. Earnest Photography; center and facing page courtesy of Rocky Mountaineer

SEWELL'S MARINA

West Coast wildlife. Superb fishing. Boating adventures. These are the sparkling gifts of the sea that make Sewell's Marina an experience not to be missed on a visit to Vancouver. When Dan Sr. and Eva Sewell and their young sons Art and Tom discovered Horseshoe Bay in 1922, the native Londoners fell in love with the port city's allure. Dan Sr., an outdoorsman and avid fisherman with a keen appreciation for nature and adventure, decided to make a home for his whole family by purchasing a small piece of waterfront property. He acquired a modest building to house his family, with hotel accommodations and a dining room for guests. Originally named Whytecliff Lodge, it served area visitors throughout the 1930s, attracting vaudevillians who would perform in local theaters at night and enjoy deep-sea fishing by day. A sport vacation destination, fishing enthusiasts were drawn to Sewell's during the '50s including celebrities like Bing Crosby, Roy Rogers, Ray Milland, and Fred McMurray. Sewell's colorful cast of characters over the years makes for great tales after a long day of boating even now.

Sewell's Marina has had several iterations since its founding. Today fourth-generation, sister-brother seafarers Megan and Eric Sewell operate the Sewell's Ocean Adventure Center at the storied marina in beautiful Howe Sound. It offers rental boats, mooring, salmon fishing charters and exciting derby events, wildlife Sea Safari adventure tours, and popular Sea Quest group scavenger hunts by boat that motivate corporate participants. Much more than a fisherman's mecca, Sewell's Marina calls to all who love the sea with fun family activities and engaging excursions to take in the scenic beauty, flora and fauna, and abundant bounty of the Pacific. Environmentally conscious stewards of the sea, Sewell's started an endangered coho and chinook salmon release program and various seal rescue teams, along with continuing charitable contributions to the Vancouver Aquarium marine science programs. Making seaworthy memories for more than 75 years, a Sewell's welcome captures Ralph Waldo Emerson's inspiring quote: "Live in the sunshine, swim the sea, drink the wild air..." as the promise of an unforgettable maritime experience beckons sea lovers everywhere.

6409 Bay Street, West Vancouver
604.921.3474 www.sewellsmarina.com

Photographs: top center, bottom left, bottom right, and facing page by Paul Yates; top left by Megan Sewell; top right by Jessica Haydahl

PADDLEWHEELER RIVERBOAT TOURS

Don't get stuck up the river without a paddlewheeler riverboat tour during your next visit to New Westminster. Along the majestic and historical Fraser River, many workboats operate amid a diversity of wildlife while history unfolds and the sun sets over breathtaking coastal mountains.

In the latter half of the 19th century, gold prospectors by the thousands rushed to British Columbia and ventured upriver on the same paddlewheelers that the company's authentic vessel, the *M.V. Native*, is modeled after. The boat's split paddle system was featured in the four-part television miniseries "Riverworld." With a background in radio broadcasting, manager Frank Froebel narrates informatively, educating passengers about the rich history of the area and the gold rush while they relax and enjoy the flowing water, gentle ride, and fine food.

A river cruise is the perfect way to relax and enjoy an event, festival, or holiday—or simply to spend a romantic evening dining and dancing with someone special.

Suite 139-810 Quayside Drive, New Westminster
604.525.4465 www.vancouverpaddlewheeler.com

Photographs: top, center right, and bottom by Valerie Iddios; center left by Louisa Bertok

SOFTBALL CITY

With spring, summer, and fall providing many excellent days for outdoor recreation, Glen Todd enjoyed coaching his daughters, both accomplished softball players. In 1987 Glen began to see the need for an outstanding softball facility for the province, so the idea for a premier sports and entertainment complex was born. Through collaboration with Softball British Columbia's president, Dale McMann, Softball City was constructed on city property in a beautiful setting surrounded by nature. The complex is now known as one of the top softball venues in Canada and a model for all of North America.

Visitors to Softball City can watch a game on any of the four championship-caliber diamonds, which host everything from major international fastpitch tournaments to slowpitch games and corporate softball events. Situated at the center of the facility is The Sports Grill, featuring enormous viewing decks that offer the perfect place to relax and observe the action.

If getting into the game is more your style, take a few swings of your own in the batting cages. The complex also offers various leagues every night of the week and tournaments every weekend throughout the entire softball season.

2201 148th Street, Surrey
604.531.3220 www.softballcity.bc.ca

Photographs courtesy of Softball City

STANLEY PARK HORSE-DRAWN TOURS

When Governor General of Canada Lord Frederick Stanley traveled to Vancouver in 1889, he explored the verdant peninsula newly dedicated as Stanley Park in a horse-drawn carriage. Mere moments away from the skyscrapers of downtown Vancouver, Stanley Park remains today a lush green expanse of vibrant rainforest, lovingly groomed flowerbeds, stunning vistas, and engaging history. Taking a horse-drawn carriage is still the best way to explore the park's thousand acres, and Stanley Park Horse-Drawn Tours provides exactly that.

Although a vital part of life in early Vancouver, horses had been absent from the park for over 30 years when company founders Gerry and Kathryn O'Neil re-established the tradition of touring the park by horse-drawn carriage. Their gentle giants now call Stanley Park home and can be seen daily meandering through majestic forest and austere monuments as they pull lightweight, environmentally friendly, hand-made carriages while riders relax to the gentle clip-clop of the horses' hooves and take in the fresh scents of cedar and the sea.

The tours offer a truly unique and memorable way to participate in a journey of discovery and unwind from the hectic pace of the city. Rich in historical information about the park, the city, and the First Nations, friendly guides provide an extraordinary storytelling adventure that will engage your imagination and forge memories to last a lifetime.

735 Stanley Park Drive, Vancouver
604.681.5115 www.stanleypark.com

Photographs: top left by Bob Warick Photography; bottom left by Ian Kim Fine Photography; right by Adrian Le Photography

TOURISM LANGLEY

A visit to the communities that make up the Langleys of British Columbia can be as versatile as the color of a chameleon. Looking for a sensory adventure? Begin with the popular Circle Farm tour—a self-guided introduction to the fresh tastes and culinary treasures of the region. Or venture to the wild side with a stroll through the Vancouver Zoo. Seeking something more relaxing? Langley is also known as the horse capital of BC, so you can enjoy world-class equestrian events or hop in the saddle yourself for a scenic trail ride through one of many spectacular park settings. Prefer to be more indulgent? Taste the offerings of the local wineries, pamper yourself in a salon or spa, peruse the quaint downtown boutiques and Village of Fort Langley specialty shops, or treat yourself to a luxurious meal at one of the area's many fine dining establishments.

With endless activities suited for all personalities and abilities and with the birthplace of British Columbia rooted in Fort Langley, boredom is sure to never cross your mind. In a place where city meets country at nearly every turn, you will want to stay and get acquainted with the possibilities, taking advantage of the accommodations that range from quaint bed and breakfasts to hotels and campsites. Whatever your fancy, Langley is sure to offer it.

7888-200th Street, Langley
604.888.1477 www.tourism-langley.ca

Photographs courtesy of Tourism Langley

THUNDERBIRD SHOW PARK

In 1966, George and Diane Tidball bought a horse for $150 at the request of their eldest daughter. Little did they know that this would be the catalyst for the family to move from their home in West Vancouver to a place more suitable for horses—Fort Langley—and open Thunderbird Equestrian Centre in 1971.

Now known as Thunderbird Show Park, the facility has become the ultimate destination for show jumping, festivals, and horse shows in the Pacific Northwest and a mecca for equine enthusiasts of all ages and disciplines. The Tidballs opened their current location, a state-of-the-art facility designed by Robert Joliecoeur of International Equestrian Design, in 1999. While horses are no longer housed on-site year-round, Thunderbird's 84 acres, three indoor arenas, and 11 outdoor rings—not to mention the par 72, 18-hole putting golf course—still provide plenty of space for visiting equestrians and excited onlookers.

Thunderbird is still a family-run business, with daughter Jane overseeing daily operations as president and granddaughter Stephanie as marketing manager. Core hospitality values ensure that what the Tidballs discovered more than 40 years ago still holds true today. You don't have to be an equestrian to feel the ground move beneath your feet, hear the rumbling of the hooves, or appreciate the amazing athleticism of the horses and riders.

24550 72nd Avenue, Langley
604.888.4585 www.thunderbirdshowpark.com

Photographs courtesy of Thunderbird Show Park

Vancouver Aquarium

When was the last time you visited an aquarium that not only displays marine life, but also seeks to engage visitors in conservation issues and solutions? And then on top of that, it pioneers new environmentally friendly techniques right in its own facilities? That's exactly what the Vancouver Aquarium does—it has transformed its own buildings into shining examples of good global citizenship. Want proof? The café's biodegradable serving ware, Ocean Wise sustainable seafood program, and a newly built LEED Gold-certified Aquaquest learning center are just a few of the ways the aquarium has made itself the greenest cultural institution cum tourist attraction in Canada.

The aquarium has come a long way from its humble origins. At a 1950 meeting of a Vancouver home aquarium society, members discussed the creation of a public aquarium, and with the additional support of the University of British Columbia zoology department, Canada's first public aquarium opened in 1956 and has grown steadily since. Dr. Murray Newman was the first curator-director of the aquarium, guiding it for 37 years until he passed the torch to current president and CEO John Nightingale in 1993.

The aquarium, which enjoys 930,000 annual visitors, aims to connect people to our natural world through a unique learning experience. Conservation, research, and education are strong themes in the 100,000-square-foot facility, which boasts multiple zones showcasing such marine denizens as beluga whales, dolphins, harbor seals, Steller sea lions, sea otters, and tropical fish, an actively connected Canada's Arctic exhibit, a café, a 4D experience theater, classrooms for school groups including a wet lab—and that's just for starters. From the curious to the passionate, guests come to explore, to learn, to watch—and come away engaged, amazed, and inspired.

845 Avison Way, Vancouver
604.659.3400 www.visitvanaqua.org

Photographs: top by Noel Hendrickson; first by Andy Wright; second and fourth by John Healey; third and fifth by Peter Holst

VANCOUVER CONVENTION CENTRE

The idea of a convention center often speaks more of function than of beauty. But the Vancouver Convention Centre is breaking traditional molds. Perched on the edge of the downtown harbor with breathtaking views of the mountains, the facility is both functional and beautiful in design, inside and out.

Covering four city blocks or 1.1 million square feet to be exact, the Vancouver Convention Centre's two connected buildings provide 471,000 square feet of flexible meeting space. Designed to open minds and feed imaginations, the west building expansion features Canada's largest waterfront ballroom and spectacular floor-to-ceiling windows to take advantage of the stunning scenery. Committed to environmental sustainability, the facility is home to the largest "living" roof in Canada with more than 400,000 indigenous plants and four beehives, as well as a marine habitat built into the foundation. The facility also utilizes a seawater heating and cooling system and runs an on-site water treatment plant. Moreover, the iconic west building has been awarded LEED Platinum certification, making this the first convention center in the world to receive the highest level of LEED designation.

The Vancouver Convention Centre was created with superb attention to detail—a characteristic also found in the extraordinary team that brings together event details seamlessly. Whether it's offering five-star culinary service from a scratch kitchen philosophy of using fresh, local, and seasonal ingredients or providing industry-leading technology with connection speeds of up to one gigabyte per second, the team always strives to exceed expectations. It's no surprise that the facility is the first-ever repeat winner of the International Association of Congress Centres' award for "World's Best Convention Centre" in 2002 and 2008.

1055 Canada Place, Vancouver
604.689.8232 www.vancouverconventioncentre.com

Photographs by Vancouver Convention Centre

VANCOUVER INTERNATIONAL AIRPORT

Just minutes from downtown, Vancouver International Airport—YVR—is Canada's second-busiest airport. Located at the crossroads of mountains, ocean, river, and city, YVR provides the first and last impression of British Columbia for thousands of travelers every day.

With inspiration from the surrounding habitat, the not-for-profit Vancouver Airport Authority—which has managed YVR since 1992—has developed an airport that reflects the inherent beauty of the West Coast. The terminals reveal views of the ocean and the mountains, and the buildings' finishing materials showcase British Columbia's natural resources.

While the award-winning art and architecture inside the airport showcase examples of traditional cultures, such as Bill Reid's *Spirit of Haida Gwaii: The Jade Canoe*, the buildings are constructed with modernity and innovation. Sustainable design elements such as solar panels, energy-efficient lighting, and motion-activated moving walkways aim to reduce the environmental impact of facilities and operations. YVR practices sustainability not only from an environmental perspective, but also through customer care and community engagement initiatives. From its award-winning Green Coat volunteer program to the Public Observation Area where locals and travelers can enjoy watching airside activity, YVR is not just an airport. It is a destination.

3211 Grant McConachie Way, Richmond
604.207.7077 www.yvr.ca

Photographs by Larry Goldstein Photography

Vancouver Lookout

Opened in 1977 by Neil Armstrong, the famous American aviator and former astronaut who was the first person to set foot on the moon, Vancouver Lookout soon became one of the premier towers in Canada, with an observation deck at 130 meters tall. When visiting British Columbia, this should be your first stop. More than 200,000 visitors from around the globe start their journey here every year.

Glass elevators on the outside of the Harbour Centre tower whisk you up to the circular deck. Spy scopes for 360-degree views provide some of the most spectacular vistas in the world, making the destination a prime venue for festive occasions of all sorts. Although the incredible day and evening panoramas of the city and environs will leave you speechless, Vancouver Lookout has even more to offer than the view. Friendly staff members lead tours in English, French, Spanish, Japanese, German, and other languages. They kindly recommend excursions, day trips, walking tours, hikes, shopping, transit options, hidden gems, ethnic neighborhoods, regional must-sees, and all kinds of well-guarded secrets. From far above the city, the knowledgeable staff can point you in directions you wouldn't find in guide books and introduce you to places where only the locals congregate.

555 West Hastings Street, Vancouver
604.689.0421 www.vancouverlookout.com

Photographs courtesy of Vancouver Lookout

THE VANCOUVER TROLLEY COMPANY

When you've had a city on your travel wish list for a while and finally get the opportunity to visit, it's easy to get caught up clicking through from flight to hotel without considering how you'll get around once you're there. You want to see the top sites and get the lay of the land without getting lost, and hopping aboard one of The Vancouver Trolley Company's turn-of-the-century replica trolleys is a great way to go.

The well-established business is owned by Jim Storie, a native Vancouverite who politely declined a promotion at a multinational corporation in favor of changing careers to stay in beautiful British Columbia. More than a decade later, he has expanded The Vancouver Trolley Company to include a few buses, a 1930 Ford convertible, and more than a dozen trolleys with two loops, 29 stops, informative and entertaining live commentary, and a casual hop-on, hop-off policy. In addition to the convenience factor, the trolleys play up the West Coast's earth-friendly mindset since they're propane-fueled—not to mention the ultimate in ridesharing.

Popular destinations like Stanley Park, Granville Island, and Vanier Park—along with tons of museums and hotspots for shopping and dining—are part of the trolley route. The company also has visitors covered for destinations off the beaten path, connecting them with various land, air, and sea tour opportunities throughout the region.

875 Terminal Avenue, Vancouver
888.451.5581 www.vancouvertrolley.com

Photographs by Kristen Macgregor

DAVISON ORCHARDS COUNTRY VILLAGE

If the scent of apple blossoms and buzz of bumblebees remind you of the simpler things in life, you're going to love Davison Orchards Country Village. It's like a trip back in time to the Okanagan's farmland known for family times and fresh air, a place of bucolic splendor where healthy fruits and vegetables are cultivated. Davison Orchards was established in 1933 on 34 acres in the Bella Vista area overlooking the town of Vernon. Tom and Tamra Davison partnered with parents Bob and Dora in 1985, sharing a vision to create a farm business offering local produce topped with a wonderful family experience. "Minutes from town, miles from ordinary," is their motto, which holds true today.

Unique apples are the specialty—like Honeycrisp, Mutsu, Gala, Fuji, and Arlet—with peaches, pumpkins, and squash right behind. Pure apple juice, delicious jams and preserves, and smooth apple and pumpkin butters are a few of the homegrown favorites you'll find in a charming country atmosphere. A bakery area is brimming with homemade pies, cookies, muffins, caramel-dipped apples, and rich fudge to satisfy any sweet tooth. Reminiscent of a farmers market with genuinely friendly people, there's Aunt May's Deep Dish Café for tasty fare. Children will surely enjoy the Johnny Popper Apple Train and Crazy Cow Kids Corral—a visit to Davison Orchards is filled with lasting memories and bushels of fun. Whether you come to celebrate harvest season at Apple Fest, October's Pumpkin Fest, or Apple Blossom Fest in May, three generations work together to promise an unforgettable day.

3111 Davison Road, Vernon
250.549.3266 www.davisonorchards.ca

Photographs: top and center left by Noah Ralston; center right and bottom by Leah Campbell

KELOWNA

A destination with something to offer every member of the family can only be Kelowna. The largest city located on the 68-mile-long Okanagan Lake, its main street ends conveniently at one of Kelowna's many beaches. That plus its parks, top-notch golf, orchards, and noteworthy wine country have put the city on the radar as one of the must-see places in British Columbia. The variety of landscapes is stunning, not to mention the lively nature of its people. Planning a weekend getaway to the heart of the Okanagan Valley is as simple as walking into the Tourism Kelowna Visitor Centre or logging on to its engaging website with up-to-the-minute information on places to stay, things to do, events schedules, and inspiring photos to help map out your trip.

Imagine relaxing in "mellow Kelowna" sipping award-winning vintages while soaking in vistas that captivate your senses. Play a round of golf on a championship course. Hit the Mission Creek Greenway by bike and gear up to hike on miles of nature trails. Make a splash enjoying summertime water sports and discover brisk winter recreation. Then there are the fine restaurants serving up creative and locally sourced cuisine, not to mention cozy bed-and-breakfasts and fragrant lavender fields awaiting your arrival. Kelowna beckons locals from British Columbia and Alberta with its unique allure, but folks from the Pacific Northwest, Ontario, and Toronto too—plus Europe—often make the annual getaway to this escape with its enchanting atmosphere and friendly faces. Guests flock to taste handcrafted reds and whites that have garnered international accolades. The Club at Tower Ranch is recognized by *Travel + Leisure* magazine and *Golf Digest*, flagging Kelowna's 17 golf courses as required stops on any golf enthusiast's tour. A favorite getaway destination, Kelowna is ripe with surprises and best-kept secrets ready to be experienced.

544 Harvey Avenue, Kelowna
800.663.4345 www.tourismkelowna.com

Photographs: top left, bottom left, and right by Brian Sprout; center left courtesy of Tourism Kelowna

KETTLE VALLEY STEAM RAILWAY

In the heart of British Columbia's Okanagan Valley, a steam locomotive still rumbles along a small section of the famous Kettle Valley Railway, showcasing an integral piece of the province's railway history.

Completed in 1916, the 325-mile-long railway opened up the southern interior of BC to the rest of Canada and its minerals and fruit to world markets. But this line was no easy feat. Although the Canadian Pacific Railway had long been present in British Columbia, no tracks had made it into the southern part of the province because of the mountainous geography. But Kettle Valley Railway president J.J. Warren and Canadian Pacific Railway magnate Sir Thomas Shaughnessy collaborated to push the railway into existence. With service connecting the area from Midway in the Kootenays to Hope in the Fraser Canyon, the line snaked its way over and around three mountain ranges—and was said to be one of the most difficult railways ever built. Included in construction was the Trout Creek Bridge, a major feature—at 619 feet long and 238 feet high, it was the third largest steel girder bridge in North America at the time.

That legacy lives on today thanks to the Kettle Valley Steam Railway, a heritage railway attraction that sees more than 25,000 visitors each year. Powered by a restored 1912 steam locomotive, it traverses the only remaining section of the historic railway. The ride takes you through the rural beauty of Summerland and over the Trout Creek Bridge, offering 90 minutes of breathtaking views, live music, and historical commentary.

18404 Bathville Road, Summerland
877.494.8424 www.kettlevalleyrail.org

Photograph by Doug Campbell

KUMSHEEN RAFTING RESORT

Water splashing everywhere, adrenaline pumping, and rapids daring its visitors to continue—this describes the rafting adventure as guided by the staff at Kumsheen Rafting Resort.

Bernie's Raft Rides, the first whitewater rafting company in British Columbia, was founded in 1973 by Bernie Fandrich, who named numerous rapids, such as the Devil's Kitchen, Garburator, and the Terminator, that are still used today. Since the first raft trip, Bernie and his family continue to be involved in day-to-day operations and have implemented impressive changes. Full resort amenities and additional guided activities are now offered. Located in Lytton where the Thompson and Fraser rivers meet, the resort was named after the Interior Salish peoples' reference to the two rivers converging as the great forks or "kumsheen."

Paddle or power rafting on the wild rivers with big waves, warm water, breathtaking scenery, and a desert-like climate is just the beginning. Guests seeking lively activities can choose from river kayaking, rock climbing, and mountain biking. A hot tub, swimming pool, and lovely accommodations—campsites, quaint tipis, and fully furnished cabin tents—are perfect for the more laid-back sightseer. Whatever the reason for a visit—to unwind or to get wound up, a day trip or multiple-night stay—the friendly, knowledgeable staff and comfortable atmosphere make this a stop not to be missed.

1345 Trans-Canada Highway, Lytton
250.455.2296 www.kumsheen.com

Photographs courtesy of Kumsheen Rafting Resort

REO RAFTING RESORT

Few activities offer the same kind of heart-pounding, adrenaline-pumping rush as whitewater rafting. Bryan Fogelman has been hooked since he bought his first boat at age 17 and started rafting the wild rivers of British Columbia. In 1989 Bryan purchased 25 acres of wilderness on the Nahatlatch River that has since become the REO Rafting Resort. Even before Bryan and his team of worldly guides put down roots, they were developing the guiding and safety skills they would later be renowned for. In 1982, Bryan and his team conducted the first-ever raft descent on the Nahatlatch River when most people still considered the river too wild for rafting.

REO's guides live, work, and play in the river valley year-round, ensuring that they know every rapid, rock, and route through the amazing Class III and IV-and-up rapids of the Nahatlatch. To help ensure that future generations will enjoy rafting in the beautiful Nahatlatch Valley, REO played an integral role in the creation of the Nahatlatch and Mehatl Provincial Parks.

In addition to the jade-green waters of the Nahatlatch, REO also takes guests down the Thompson, Nicola, Taseko, Chilko, Fraser, Coquihalla, and Stein rivers. Each varies in its degree of difficulty, but all include the breathtaking snow-capped peaks, rich forest, and sheer canyon walls that surround the waterways. If having knuckles as white as the rapids doesn't entice, REO also offers canyon rappelling, rock climbing, kayaking, and hiking to the spectacular Mehatl Falls. At the end of each adventure, the option of a relaxing hot tub soak or an aromatherapy massage awaits. Finish each day sitting around a campfire and falling asleep to the sound of whitewater in your own personal river's edge tent cabin—a truly unique experience.

Boston Bar
604.461.7238 www.reorafting.com

Photographs by Ryan Robinson

Sun Peaks Resort

An adventurous and charming alpine community, Sun Peaks Resort, located in the North Thompson region of British Columbia, is a four-season, award-winning destination. Originally Tod Mountain, a locals' ski hill since 1961, commercial development of Sun Peaks began in 1993 and has bestowed the community with world-class status. Olympic gold medalist and Canada's Female Athlete of the 20th Century Nancy Greene calls Sun Peaks home and was key in the resort's development, showcasing its caliber.

A Tyrolean-inspired pedestrian village greets guests with cobblestone walkways in the summer and ski-through convenience in the winter. The village is home to boutique shops, plus cafés and restaurants that offer diverse culinary options, many using local ingredients. Accommodations range from comfortable to high-end, ideal for any budget. As Canada's third-largest ski area, Sun Peaks has three mountains of terrain on 3,678 acres. Moderate temperatures offer a pleasant winter experience with dry powder, famous to this region of BC. Non-skiers enjoy dog sledding,

snowshoeing, snowmobiling, ice skating, tubing, horse-drawn sleigh rides, and the spa.

The summer months are a hiker's paradise, with lift-accessed hiking on Tod Mountain where indigenous wildflowers, like arctic lupine and Indian paintbrush, bloom. Thrill seekers can try the lift-accessed Bike Park with 70 kilometers of trails. At the base, the 18-hole Graham Cooke-designed golf course hosts the highest tee in BC—#16 at 4,000 feet!

Looking for the perfect chance to visit? Take advantage of the abundant festivals and celebrations the resort holds, including the Winter Festival of Wine, BC Family Day Celebration, and Autumn Bounty.

Suite 13-3250 Village Way, Sun Peaks
250.578.5399 www.sunpeaksresort.com

Photographs by Adam Stein

TWIN ANCHORS HOUSEBOATS

Imagine being rocked to sleep by gentle waves, lulled into a relaxing state in a luxurious bed. Then, envision the excitement of waking up refreshed with just a few steps necessary to jump in the water, sunbathe on the roof, or watch a bit of TV before capping off the day with a drink in the swim-up bar—and all of this while surrounded by stunning scenery. Sound too good to be true?

At Twin Anchors Houseboats, this scenario happens every day on one of the more than 100 houseboats. More accurately described as the ultimate floating resorts, each home-away-from-home sleeps from two to 24 people and has ample space to relax. Hesitant to leave your own amenities behind? No problem. All of the houseboats feature a grill and kitchen with all appliances and utensils, a television, a waterslide, a fireplace, and a hot tub; some even include air conditioning, a gaming system, a washer and dryer, and a steam shower.

With marinas in Sicamous and Salmon Arm, Twin Anchors provides an excellent way to see and experience the wild and rugged Shuswap Lake, aptly named Canada's houseboating paradise with its pristine, sandy beaches, towering waterfalls, and warm, clear water.

101 Martin Street, Sicamous
800.663.4026 www.twinanchors.com

Photographs courtesy of Twin Anchors Houseboats

ABBOTSFORD

Do you prefer the quiet countryside or are you the proverbial city slicker? You can experience the best of both worlds in Abbotsford, a unique destination aptly nicknamed "The City in the Country." People who visit Abbotsford are so inspired by its vibrant atmosphere that many decide to live, work, and play here, making it one of the fastest growing cities in British Columbia. Only 40 minutes from Vancouver, nestled in the verdant Fraser Valley with historic roots from the Gold Rush era, Abbotsford has all of the amenities of a modern city right in the middle of one of Canada's most beautiful and bountiful agricultural areas.

Abbotsford's natural splendor and diverse culture capture everyone who lands here. Spectacular mountain peaks, sparkling lakes, flowing rivers, and open green spaces surround the city, creating a magical place. It's an eclectic blend of trendsetting urban style and friendly country living with a broad range of activities. The exciting Abbotsford Entertainment & Sports Centre and The Reach Gallery Museum are just a few of the community's key attractions. Experience the adrenaline rush of skydiving, unwind at a spa, take in the thrills of the Abbotsford International Airshow, dine at over 200 restaurants, attend sporting events, concerts, and heritage festivals, or simply enjoy down-home music in the farmers' market. Mere minutes from downtown, the Abbotsford International Airport is the city's main hub serving all of British Columbia with daily flights, so getting here is a breeze and staying a while is sure to please.

32315 South Fraser Way, Abbotsford
604.853.2281 www.abbotsford.ca

Photographs courtesy of the City of Abbotsford

BARKERVILLE NATIONAL HISTORIC SITE

When Billy Barker struck gold on Williams Creek in 1862, he probably couldn't have predicted how many thousands of international prospectors would travel great distances for a shot at getting rich. Barkerville boomed between 1862 and 1870, with more than 100,000 people arriving via the Cariboo Wagon Road to work in the goldfields.

Barkerville was once a bustling city filled with traffic, people, excitement, and optimism, and it didn't take long to become the largest city west of Chicago and north of San Francisco. The historic town of Barkerville is now BC's largest living museum and hosts more than 65,000 guests throughout the summer. Walk down the streets where miners once walked, take a stagecoach ride, and interact with the costumed interpretive staff.

The Chinese community was an integral part of Barkerville life for nearly 100 years. They established a number of businesses, including the Kwong Lee Company, a general store that sold groceries, clothing, hardware, and mining tools. The Chinese community also built cabins for Chinese miners, the Chee Kung Tong Chinese Freemason's Hall, and the Tai Ping Fong—"Peace Room"—a nursing facility for the elderly.

Visiting Barkerville is like going back in time, with more than 125 heritage buildings, live theater, and educational demonstrations. History will truly come to life as you explore what Barkerville has to offer.

Barkerville
888.994.3332 www.barkerville.ca

Photographs by Thomas Drasdauskis

Harrison Hot Springs

Hop in the car and drive out to Harrison Hot Springs, where you'll "find nature just up the road," as the town's motto goes. This legendary village is located only 90 minutes from Vancouver and just a three-hour drive straight north from Seattle. The perfect vacation spot and getaway, the quaint and romantic place was discovered in 1850 by Salish settlers. Two natural hot springs, Sulphur Spring and Potash Spring, soon became revered healing places, drawing locals and visitors to therapeutic mineral-rich waters. A wonderful place to unwind, steamy pools attract health-conscious guests today, and the experience of its deeply relaxing, 100-degree healing baths is not to be missed.

Nestled along pristine Harrison Lake, outdoor recreation abounds from water activities, boating, swimming, and fishing to hiking, snow sports, and great golf. If the pulse of adventure runs through your veins, salmon and sturgeon fishing is top-notch; plus exciting stock car racing is nearby for those with the need for speed. Full-service resorts and spas roll out the red carpet for everyone looking to escape their busy lives and get back to nature; fine accommodations at the end of a full day spell relaxation in comfortable and luxurious style. Harrison Hot Springs is a year-round destination. Enjoy winter skiing amid great mountain scenery in the snowy months, discover summer family fun, concerts, events, and local festivals throughout the warmer months, or plan a cycling trip as majestic trees don their autumn hues. You're cordially invited to historic Harrison Hot Springs to experience it all—the beauty of nature, lake tours, and entertainment, with plenty of leisurely shopping and dining.

499 Hot Springs Road, Harrison Hot Springs
604.796.5581 www.tourismharrison.com

Photographs: top courtesy of Harrison Hot Springs Resort & Spa; bottom and right courtesy of Tourism Harrison

HELL'S GATE AIRTRAM

Although explorer Simon Fraser reported that he had "encountered the gates of hell" when he scaled the canyon walls along the Fraser River in 1808, it simply feels like an exciting, fun adventure to take in that same scenery while safely aboard a Hell's Gate Airtram. This locally owned and operated attraction sponsors many local organizations, such as the Fraser Canyon Hospice Society, and hosts seasonal events that are immensely enjoyable for locals and visitors alike.

The excursion departs from highway level on a spacious tram that descends over Hell's Gate—the narrowest part of the Fraser River at only 33 meters wide, boasting twice the volume of Niagara Falls' water—and the International Fishways, which assist the millions of salmon each year that journey home to their spawning grounds. Before the trams ascend back to highway level, a stop at the lower terminal offers a suspension bridge, education center, café with mouthwatering salmon chowder, a decadent fudge and ice cream shop, and gold panning activities to engage each visitor.

43111 Trans-Canada Highway, Boston Bar
604.867.9277 www.hellsgateairtram.com

Photographs courtesy of Hell's Gate Airtram

Tourism Kamloops

The city of Kamloops certainly lives up to its name, but it offers much more than that. Its moniker is derived from the word "tk'emlúps" from the Secwepemc people—a semi-nomadic nation who settled in the area and gave the name of "where the rivers meet," referring to the convergence of the North and South Thompson rivers. Most assuredly Kamloops provides a meeting place for many types of activities, especially with its central location in the southern interior, poised to connect with Vancouver, Calgary, and Edmonton.

But Kamloops is more than just a hub. As "Canada's Tournament Capital," it's a place to let your hair down and just enjoy yourself. With more than 2,000 hours of sunshine annually and a vast, rugged landscape with a variety of terrain, the outdoor activities are endless. Golf, mountain biking, wildlife viewing—including the BC Wildlife Park—rockhounding, hiking, year-round fishing, downhill skiing and Sun Peaks Resort's other offerings, dog sledding, snowshoeing, sleigh riding, and snowmobiling are just the beginning. A three-day cowboy festival, pro and amateur rodeos, and the beautifully restored Kamloops Heritage Railway's 2141 steam locomotive take people back to a time when train robberies and the Gold Rush were more than just stories. For an indoors experience, disco bowling, rock climbing gyms, the Big Little Science Center, a casino, theaters, symphony, and the Sunmore Ginseng Spa—North America's only ginseng spa—will keep the enjoyment level at an all-time high.

While visiting, don't forget to ask about the legends of the Balancing Rock, the Strangest Newspaper in the World, and the ghost of Walhachin, and be sure to journey to the Center of the Universe. Whatever your budget or style, Kamloops is a great place to let loose and just play.

1290 West Trans-Canada Highway, Kamloops
250.372.8000 www.tourismkamloops.com

Photographs: top and bottom by Kelly Funk; second by Tyler Meade; third by Tobiano/Bob Huxtable

RADIUM HOT SPRINGS

When the weather's freezing cold, a relaxing soak in steaming water sounds nearly irresistible. Not only does the resort community of Radium Hot Springs, with its odorless natural hot springs, prove enticing for winter visitors, its proximity to lakes, golf courses, national parks, and other nature attractions makes it a spectacular draw year-round.

Located at the south entrance of Kootenay National Park—on the Columbia River, between the Rocky Mountain and Purcell Mountain ranges—the mountain getaway village veritably hums with activities, special events, and attractions for every season of the year. Visitor-friendly, a variety of accommodations and dining spots await those seeking an exciting, fun, outdoorsy destination. And don't forget the breathtaking views; the mountainous location provides the village with 360-degree alpine scenery.

In addition to the star attraction—the hot springs mineral pools surrounded by natural rock walls—there's the Columbia River Wetlands, the longest continuous wetlands in North America and an excellent bird watching area with more than 300 species. Nature will be at your door: A herd of about 150 bighorn sheep winter in the community and take over the town from September to May as they block traffic, eat flowers, and graze on lawns and golf greens. Golfers and skiers will find much to love in the two courses in town and a dozen more within 45 minutes—including several championship courses—as well as three ski resorts only a short drive away featuring cross-country and snowmobiling. As if that weren't enough, there's also mini golf, trail riding, fishing, go-carting, hiking, whitewater rafting, and canoeing, plus shopping and dining for those who prefer less athletic adventures. From natural scenery and wildlife to a wealth of outdoor activities to fine dining and accommodations, Radium Hot Springs brims with attractions for everyone.

Radium Hot Springs
250.347.9331 www.radiumhotsprings.com

Photographs: top Dale Genest; bottom and right by Bram Rossman

SUNSHINE COAST TOURISM

Exciting. Relaxing. Beautiful. Natural. The Sunshine Coast is breathtakingly picturesque with snow-capped mountains, seaside cliffs running along the Pacific, rainforests, and glacier-sculpted fjords, as well as some of the most scenic hiking trails in Canada. Attracting outdoor adventurers worldwide, it also has a softer side with the most artist residents per capita in BC and year-round festivals in every genre from writing to music to fine art. Canada has a lot to be proud of, but the Sunshine Coast is perhaps its star. Friendly oceanside towns welcome you to the coast, including Gibsons—named the Best Community in the World by the UN-endorsed LivCom Awards—and Powell River, anointed the Cultural Capital of Canada in 2004.

So if mountain biking, hiking, kayaking, sailing, rock climbing, swimming, and diving appeal to you, or if festivals of jazz, Celtic, chamber music, blues, folk, and chorale get you going, and if painters, sculptors, glass blowers, jewelry designers, and carvers delight you, then you have reached paradise here. The Sunshine Coast extends along the Strait of Georgia from Howe Sound to Desolation Sound. Myriad waterways, coastal mountains, old-growth forests, and deep seas draw international visitors to ride Skookumchuck Narrows' tidal rapids, enjoy nature's majesty, scuba alongside a bronze mermaid, and explore World War II ships. Romance lives on the Sunshine Coast too. Charming bed-and-breakfasts dot the region, as do wonderful resorts and guest lodges with pampering spas to take your cares away.

111-4871 Joyce Avenue, Powell River
604.485.4701 www.sunshinecoastcanada.com

Photographs: top by Kelly Funk; bottom and right by Darren Robinson Photography

WILLIAMS LAKE

Cowboy. This term often connotes a horseback-riding, hat-wearing, strong, rugged, loyal man that is honest and full of character. While this traditional icon may be losing popularity in younger generations, there's at least one place where the good ol' cowboy is respected and revered.

Named the stampede capital of British Columbia, the city of Williams Lake has rightly preserved a delightful frontier atmosphere. The annual stampede—one of the largest in North America—portrays western charm through activities such as the Pony Express race, wild cow milking, and team cattle penning, while the Cowboy Hall of Fame honors the greats of the past.

It's not all about the cowboy, though. Known as the Shangri-La of mountain biking, the region offers an abundance of outdoor activities. The city is a launch pad to diverse landscapes and cultures—where you can go from desert to rainforest within an hour's drive and learn about the heritage of First Nations and the gold rush along the way. The day simply isn't long enough to see and do it all, so the best bet is to start at the Tourism Discovery Centre. From there, the cowboy—and a myriad of other interests—are available to discover.

Williams Lake
877.967.5253 www.williamslake.ca

Photographs: top and bottom courtesy of the City of Williams Lake; center and facing page by Chris Harris

Guild House Antiques, page 127

Chali-Rosso Art Gallery, page 125

Vancouver Civic Theatres, page 136

Sasha Beliaev and Lena Rivkina, page 133

Ian Tan Gallery, page 130

Marion Scott Gallery, page 131

Seymour Art Gallery, page 134

APPRECIATE

ARTS & CULTURE

Behold. Ponder. Observe. From shows and concerts to plays and performances, British Columbia is a hub of arts and culture. A staggering number of museums, art galleries, theaters, concert halls, and cultural institutions offer an endless supply of activities for the arts-minded individual and anyone seeking a feast for the eyes and the mind. Talented artists, intriguing galleries, festivals, and theaters delight through appreciable creations and fascinating artistic philosophies.

ART GLASS DESIGN

Imagine plain, flat glass pieces transformed into contemporary works of art you can eat on. That's exactly what designer Jane Mackay had in mind in the early '80s. She discovered a closeout on flat, greenish-colored glass, so the inspired artist bought 2,000 square feet of the exciting new medium, with an ingenious idea to make special kiln-fired glassware. Her bright studio boasts dinnerware, serving ware, sectional platters, trays, and bowls. The unique line of simple, geometric glass dishes has captured the attention of professional chefs and anyone who appreciates functional, versatile, durable, and beautiful art glass for serving colorful food with smart style.

The founder of Art Glass Design has been working with glass material for more than 30 years, always fascinated by its amazing metamorphosis when fired at intense heat. Although largely self-taught, Jane studied glass-making techniques at Dale Chihuly's respected Pilchuck Glass School in Washington State, The Studio at The Corning Museum of Glass, Alfred University in New York, and Red Deer College in Alberta. Art Glass Design is the brand name behind Jane's handcrafted collection of original glass designs.

Jane's reputation for creating high quality and timeless collectibles has sparked a following for Art Glass Design pieces. Computer-controlled kilns ensure precise firing temperatures so that each piece is a strong, dishwasher-safe, microwaveable work of art. Edges are refined and perfectly polished using an exclusive technique that gives a uniform satin finish. Art glass pieces can also be custom-engraved as personalized gifts. For the final touch, a golden artist's mark is applied to identify each creation as an authentic E. Jane Mackay Art Glass Design collectible.

22416-129 Avenue, Maple Ridge
888.894.5277 www.artglassdesign.com

Photographs courtesy of Art Glass Design

BARBARA BOLDT'S STUDIO

Poets creatively use their imaginative and expressive faculties in relation to the written or spoken word. Barbara Boldt, in a similar fashion, embraces those capabilities with pastel, oil, and watercolor to fashion original works of art—visual poems. Inspired by Henry David Thoreau's belief in focusing on the existing world for fear of becoming alienated from reality, she paints in a realist style. Barbara often hones in on nature to capture her essence and fully respect all she has to offer. With series such as Earth Patterns and For the Love of Trees, Barbara marvels at nature's perfection and preserves landscapes to ensure they can be enjoyed forever.

After years of appreciating art in her native Germany and then in Canada, Barbara found herself an empty-nester with time on her hands. An ad for art lessons by Aeron McBryde of Maple Ridge caught Barbara's eye;

Barbara fully realized the importance of expressing herself visually. After three years of in-depth studying, Barbara opened her first commercial gallery in 1981. Now, at the age of 80, Barbara has become a respected artist and was even the first living artist to be showcased in the Fort Langley Museum. She allows others to see nature through her eyes at her home studio and gallery and imparts her accumulated knowledge and skill through oil and pastel classes.

25340 84th Avenue, Langley
604.888.5490 www.barbaraboldt.com

Paintings by Barbara Boldt

BARD ON THE BEACH SHAKESPEARE FESTIVAL

"All the world's a stage," declares Shakespeare in *As You Like It*. This could not be truer for the annual Bard on the Beach Shakespeare Festival, which has been staging performances in Vanier Park against one of the most naturally beautiful seaside backdrops imaginable for more than 20 years.

Held annually from June through September, the festival that celebrates the work of William Shakespeare draws on a dynamic team of professional actors, directors, and designers—plus more than 200 highly trained volunteers helping to carry out the event's mandate of "affordable, accessible" Shakespeare.

Beyond the performances, the festival takes Shakespeare into the community with its Bard Education programs. In addition to Young Shakespeareans summer workshops for youths and teens and Student Matinees viewed by over 250 schools, Bard offers off-season seminars for kids and teachers alike.

The grounds feature two performance tents and a Bard Village with a bar, concessions, and gift areas all providing service to the Mainstage tent's 520 patrons and the Studio Stage venue's 240. Rising from its humble beginnings, Bard has seen both local and tourist attendance grow steadily and plans to expand its capacity accordingly. The festival hopes to share the magic of Shakespeare with no less than 100,000 theater lovers in the years to come.

1695 Whyte Avenue, Vancouver
877.739.0559 www.bardonthebeach.org

Facing page: The Comedy of Errors *2009, Gord Myron, Christopher Gaze (festival's artistic director), Luc Roderique, and Amber Lewis; photographs by David Blue*

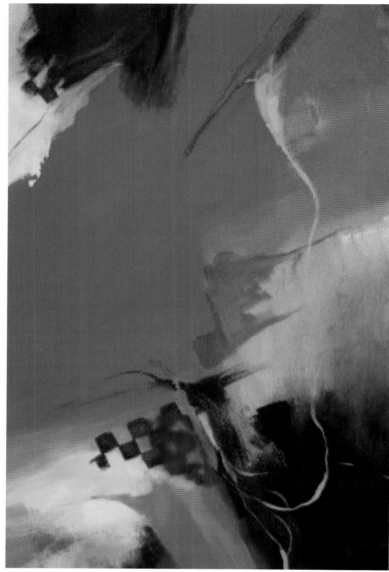

BRONWYN WILLIAMS

For Bronwyn Williams, art is an exploration for a universal and eternal expression that spans many cultures and periods of time. Our ability to connect with art of such vastly different origins inspires her work.

As a Canadian with an Australian heritage and a background in science, medicine, and music, Bronwyn has a diverse creative repository that fuels her visual and heartfelt exploration.

While working in an abstract style, she is also interested in searching for a contemporary approach to represent the human form and has produced an expansive collection of works on canvas and paper.

Influenced by her father and grandfather, who were both artists, Bronwyn has a fascination with color, shape, and line and a joy of playing with paint.

Vancouver
604.875.8348 www.bronwynwilliams.com

Paintings by Bronwyn Williams

CHALI-ROSSO ART GALLERY

Developed in the 20th century, surrealism—a style of visual art and literature that stresses the subconscious through fantastic imagery and an incongruous juxtaposition of subject matter—has its roots in anti-World War I sentiments, almost as a way of rebelling against the "rationalism" that culminated in the horrors of the war. Surrealism renounced logic and realism, overturning the social and cultural conventions of the time. With amazing art created by people like Arp, Chagall, Dalí, Magritte, Ernst, and Miró, the movement had fascinating effects on the art world.

A love for surrealist art was only the beginning for Susanna Strem and her husband, Zoltan Kulley; soon they had devoted their entire lives to antiques and art in Europe, the birthplace of surrealism. In 2005, they opened a gallery in Vancouver to showcase and sell original graphic works by 20th-century surrealist artists. Inspired by a few particular artists—namely Chagall, Dalí, Miró, and Picasso—the gallery name was created using letters from each of the artists' last names.

The unpretentious, airy showroom in South Granville seems almost humble—until the artists' names are read. With pieces from the likes of Renoir, Rembrandt, Matisse, Picasso, Braque, and Warhol, the gallery features artwork that speaks to the heart and soul.

2250 Granville Street, Vancouver
604.733.3594 www.chalirosso.com

Top and bottom photographs courtesy of Chali-Rosso Art Gallery; center original lithograph, Le Printemps, *by Marc Chagall, 1961*

COASTAL PEOPLES FINE ARTS GALLERY

Similar to other aboriginal and indigenous groups in colonized regions, the First Nations and Inuit peoples of Canada have felt the effects of integration for many years. However, with inspiration and the creation of their art, these groups and their works have become recognized as culturally significant and valued for display and acquisition. It's fortunate that there are places, such as Coastal Peoples Fine Arts Gallery, which strive to bring First Nations and Inuit art to the forefront of North American and international minds by showcasing a contemporary Northwest Coast collection.

Founders and partners Svetlana Fouks and Raymond Kazemzadeh, educated in art and culture, established the Yaletown gallery in 1996 to provide seasoned and new collectors with this historically significant art form. She believes it is imperative to view cultures through the eyes of the indigenous peoples and to experience the mythologies and stories behind their art. Her pride lies in having created a space that educates, shares, and preserves their rich heritage.

Within restored warehouse settings, both the Yaletown and Gastown galleries feature a monumental collection of such objets d'art as fine jewelry, argillite, cedar wood ceremonial masks, bent boxes, totems, basketry, glass, prints, original paintings, sculptures, reference books, and more. Ultimately, the gallery is considered a leader in recognizing emerging talent and representing British Columbia's master artisans.

1024 Mainland Street, Vancouver
312 Water Street, Vancouver
604.685.9298 www.coastalpeoples.com

Photographs by Kenji Nagai

GUILD HOUSE ANTIQUES

Mantel clock chimes strike the hour at varying times while soft music plays. The mood is elegant and relaxing at Guild House Antiques, an emporium specializing in English and continental 17th-, 18th-, and 19th-century furniture and objets d'art. Wandering the shop is like a sophisticated treasure hunt—the showroom is filled to the brim with historical pieces that are handpicked and well-presented.

Proprietors Ivar and Janice Fossen have been retailers of unique antiques for over 30 years; their shop is situated in prestigious Gallery Row on Vancouver's renowned Granville Street. The collection of imported finds covers two floors and over 4,000 square feet, offering a wide array of antique furniture and furnishings and vintage decorative accessories. It's akin to visiting your well-to-do grandmother's attic where something wonderful is discovered around every corner. The knowledgeable dealer-couple travels around the world acquiring antiques of great quality, and each piece is tagged with a description, dated, and authenticated as being more than 100 years old, which is the European standard for identifying a true antique. One-of-a-kind pieces are lovingly cleaned, waxed, and cared for, ready for their next appreciative owner.

The boutique is a member of LAPADA, the prestigious association of art and antique dealers in London, England, so shoppers can rest assured that Guild House Antiques are certifiably the best.

2121 Granville Street, Vancouver
604.739.2141 www.guildhouseantiques.com

Photographs by H. Steven Bridge

ie Creative Artworks

No trip to the artsy Granville Island community is complete without a stop at ie Creative Artworks. Designed to reflect the nature of the company, the building looks like creative chaos. Producing works of art that are beautiful, engaging, and site-specific, artists create in full view of passersby in an atmosphere of laid back industriousness.

The cofounders established the business in 1994. Trained in nuclear physics, Michael Vandermeer is a sculptor with a remarkable aptitude for engineering, metallurgy, electronics, and chemistry. Conceptual artist Cheryl Hamilton designs with a kineticism inspired by her education as an animator at Vancouver's Emily Carr Institute. They collaborate on all designs, using ideas that interest and complement them both, and they are increasingly receiving commissions for sculptures across North America.

Inspired by the communities in which their art is displayed, Michael and Cheryl work with engineers and administrators to ensure their artwork meets the requirements for building codes and regulations. Though they create artwork of all sizes, they have extensive experience with the processes and intricacies of creating large-scale public art of stainless steel, glass, and bronze, which is gratifying for the materials' aesthetic and archival qualities.

1399 Railspur Alley, Vancouver
604.254.4374 www.iecreative.ca

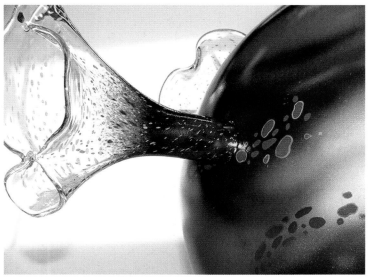

Photographs by Michael Vandermeer

IAN TAN GALLERY

With an affinity for beautiful Canadian art and a passion for hand-blown glass sculpture, Ian Tan founded his namesake gallery in prestigious South Granville's Gallery Row. His welcoming exhibition space represents works created by more than 25 British Columbia artists. Offering original art in various mediums, the contemporary gallery allows art appreciators and collectors to explore new visual concepts in an unhurried, refined environment conducive to art-gazing.

The chic gallery showcases and promotes established and emerging Canadian talent specializing in two- and three-dimensional, contemporary fine artwork, including painting, glass, ceramics, bronze sculpture, and photography. Many of the gallery's exclusive artists are drawn to Vancouver's unrivaled beauty and depict themes found in nature.

Renowned for discovering up-and-coming artists, Ian brings new talent into the limelight so others can acquire such imaginative work. Immersed in the world of art, Ian has developed a keen eye for choosing sensitive and relevant contemporary creations. He values the personal relationships with each artisan to better convey the method and meaning behind every piece lining his gallery walls. Visiting one-on-one with the gallery owner, guests gain valuable insight into an artist's unique style, inspirations, and techniques. And the gallery's monthly special exhibition openings offer the opportunity to meet an artist and learn about his or her engaging studio perspectives, not to mention the chance to enjoy lively conversation with fellow art-lovers.

2202 Granville Street, Vancouver
604.738.1077 www.iantangallery.com

Paintings and photographs: top center by Patty Ampleford; top right by Suzy Kim; bottom left by John Beder; bottom center by David Wilson; bottom right by Eri Ishii; top left by Mark Faviell

MARION SCOTT GALLERY

Marion Scott Gallery is one of those rare and unique art venues dedicated to showcasing little-known independent artists over big-name Old Masters. In the case of this gallery it's fine Inuit art, which serves to raise awareness and expose gallery guests to these noteworthy yet geographically remote artists native to Canada's northern regions.

Inspired by a chance meeting with art dealer Theo Waddington, Marion Scott organized the first major exhibition of Inuit sculpture on the West Coast at the Vancouver Hotel in 1966. Marion eventually opened her own Vancouver gallery in 1975. The gallery sold Matisse and Picasso paintings initially, but now it focuses on the very best of northern art, both contemporary and older. Marion's daughter Judy Scott Kardosh took over in 1989 and guides the gallery in its production of major, fully curated educational exhibitions and permanent installations of high-quality Inuit sculpture, prints, drawings, and wall-hangings. Thanks to the gallery, a mature market for Inuit art has developed among patrons, and a constant Inuit presence has been introduced into the city's cultural life.

Now located in Vancouver's Gastown district, the gallery is a bright, airy space with cedar beams and a loft feel. The Marion Scott Gallery not only exhibits its Inuit artists' work but also brings the artists themselves into the city to teach firsthand about the importance of indigenous art. And thanks to the curatorial co-direction of third-generation family member Robert Kardosh, the gallery publishes exhibition-related catalogues and books on northern art, helping to further develop the body of critical writing on Inuit art and artists.

308 Water Street, Vancouver
604.685.1934 www.marionscottgallery.com

Left photograph courtesy of Marion Scott Gallery; all other photographs by Trevor Mills; top center stonecut print, Festive Bird, *by Pitseolak Ashoona; bottom center serpentinite sculpture,* Tired Woman, *by Oviloo Tunnillie; right top wool textile art with brass and beads,* The Fall of K'iid K'iyaas, *by Hazel Wilson; right bottom stone sculpture,* Untitled, *by John Pangnark*

SASHA BELIAEV AND LENA RIVKINA

Art is more than just an amusing pastime for Sasha Beliaev and Lena Rivkina. It is their life's passion. First acquainted while they were studying classical art—18th- and 19th-century architecture, academic drawing, painting, and sculpting—at Moscow Architectural Institute in Russia, husband-and-wife team Sasha and Lena have since developed their own amazing portfolios.

Sasha and Lena's career highlights began in Paris working as assistants with stage designer Ezio Frigerio and Oscar-winning costume designer Franca Squarciapino. After assisting on more than 70 productions, Sasha and Lena became set and costume designers for numerous productions at highly esteemed theaters around the world; they were even commissioned by Placido Domingo for the 100th anniversary of *Tosca*.

Their mission is a quest for beauty, both with their move to Vancouver and with their desire to paint—Lena with oils and Sasha in the digital medium. With such stunning surroundings and lovely atmosphere, Sasha and Lena are fulfilling their dreams and working to spread beauty to others.

Vancouver
778.772.4667 www.scrawnypaws.com

Paintings: above, Still Life with Pomegranates, *by Lena Rivkin, 2009; facing page,* The Fearsome Pyrate Cascabel aka Arthur Whittam, *by Sasha Beliaev, 2007*

Seymour Art Gallery

Founded by a group of North Vancouver residents and artists in 1985, Seymour Art Gallery is a nonprofit, charitable public community gallery that is committed to further developing the arts and pushing the creative envelope and expectations of the community.

As part of its mandate, the gallery provides exhibitions in all media, establishing high standards in the visual and performing arts, as well as playing an educational role in art appreciation for the public and schools.

Seymour Art Gallery, located in the quaint little community of Deep Cove, hosts about 13 exhibits per year—primarily local artists and a few international guests. Individual artists are promoted in exhibits that are often combined with the performing arts to create a wonderful multi-dimensional experience. One of the gallery's more successful education programs is "Creative Lives Lived," a series where local artists talk about their lives and art. The gallery hosts a number of annual and biannual events; its popular June festival event features eight artists per week for five consecutive weeks with related performances in an upbeat atmosphere. Housed in a heritage-style building that blends in nicely with the seaside feel of Deep Cove, the gallery also offers a gift shop featuring items handmade by British Columbia artisans.

4360 Gallant Avenue, North Vancouver
604.924.1378 www.seymourartgallery.com

Photographs: top and bottom left by Andrew Chamberlayne; center and bottom right by Tina Schliessler; facing page courtesy of Seymour Art Gallery

VANCOUVER CIVIC THEATRES

In terms of the performing arts, Vancouver could be considered a visionary city in part because it owns and operates three theaters—the Queen Elizabeth, the Playhouse, and the Orpheum—and supports the arts with cultural grants up to $10 million annually.

The city built the Queen Elizabeth Theatre, opened in 1959, and the Vancouver Playhouse, opened in 1962. In 1973, the Orpheum—the oldest of the theaters, originally built in 1927 for vaudeville—was closed and slated for demolition. When citizens banded together, launching a save-the-theater campaign, the city purchased the theater and reopened it in 1977.

All three theaters have benefited from major renovations, from acoustic and sound system upgrades to new lighting systems and upgraded seating. Collectively the theaters are known as Vancouver Civic Theatres, and they hold about 700 events per year, including performances by the Vancouver Symphony, Vancouver Opera, Playhouse Theatre Company, Ballet British Columbia, Friends of Chamber Music, DanceHouse, Vancouver Recital Society, and Vancouver Bach Choir. Whether hosting an intimate show or an extravagant production, each venue offers patrons a unique experience.

649 Cambie Street, Vancouver
604.665.3050 www.vancouver.ca/theatres

Photographs: top and bottom by Ed White; facing page by Martin Knowles

SUSANNA BLUNT

If you think you're not familiar with the artwork of Susanna Blunt, take a quick look inside your coin purse. The portrait of H.M. Queen Elizabeth II that has adorned every Canadian coin since 2003 was created by Susanna, one of nine invited artists who competed to design the monarch's new likeness. Susanna, a portrait artist who also specializes in sculptures, murals, and trompe-l'œil, has cultivated throughout her career a vast clientele that spans the globe.

A Canadian native, Susanna always knew she would become an artist. After first attending the Banff School of Fine Arts in Canada, she graduated from a three-year diploma course at the Byam Shaw School of Art in London, England, and was then awarded a four-year scholarship to the Royal Academy of Arts. Teaching positions in California and Vancouver followed, but like a true artist, Susanna has traveled the world for her subjects. She has worked previously with Yoko Ono, painted a portrait of Prince Edward that she personally delivered to Buckingham Palace,

and was chosen in a nationwide competition by Gerda Hnatyshyn, wife of the Canadian Governor General, to paint her portrait for Rideau Hall in Ottawa, Ontario.

Susanna sees herself as an explorer, someone who discovers what materials, textures, and colors will do when combined, as opposed to an artist who expresses her own thoughts and emotions. "That," according to Susanna, "would be boring."

Vancouver
604.926.5078 www.bluntart.com

Art by Susanna Blunt: top left mixed media sculpture, Messenger; *bottom left oil and acrylic on canvas,* Trompe L'œil Tiger; *bottom right oil and acrylic on canvas,* Trompe L'œil Drill Bit; *top right oil painting on canvas,* Portrait of Christian; *photographs by B.J. Clayden*

VANCOUVER CHAMBER CHOIR

The Vancouver Chamber Choir is all about preserving choral masterworks of the past and creating the new choral traditions of the future. Since the choir's first performance in 1971, conductor Jon Washburn has endeavored to convey the vitality and beauty of choral music both new and old.

Jon's love for music began at an early age as part of a musical family. Through his education and experience in a wide variety of styles—classical, jazz, folk, and popular—this love became a surpassing passion. For him, a professional choir serves as the perfect instrument to express the joy of song to his audiences.

As British Columbia's most-traveled large ensemble, the choir has undertaken 80 tours in its 40-year history, 20 of those international. Each year they present up to 50 performances and educational outreach events, including an extensive 10-concert subscription series in Vancouver. Their immense repertoire supports Canadian composers and performers in a way that is second-to-none. Music lovers—from students to choral devotees to musical visitors—always come away impressed with the Vancouver Chamber Choir's mastery and articulation within the wide world of the choral art.

1254 West 7th Avenue, Vancouver
604.738.6822 www.vancouverchamberchoir.com

Photographs: top left by Mishiro; top center and right by Dave Roels; bottom by Howard Meharg

VANCOUVER PLAYHOUSE THEATRE COMPANY

As its 50th anniversary nears, the Vancouver Playhouse Theatre Company is reinventing itself. Conceived in 1962 as Vancouver's premier regional professional theater, the Playhouse has built a reputation around showcasing local and international talent and developing world premieres such as *The Overcoat* and *The Ecstasy of Rita Joe*. The appointment of artistic managing director Max Reimer in 2008 has translated into an exciting new direction for the company—starting with lifting the restriction of only producing plays written after 1950.

Besides embracing both contemporary plays and the classics, the Playhouse now rounds out its program with a big splashy musical during the winter holidays. Broadway hits *The Drowsy Chaperone* and *Dirty Rotten Scoundrels* have both been wildly successful in past seasons, and Max promises more toe-tapping music and eye-popping choreography in the years to come.

Perhaps in imitation of the perennial nomads of show business, the company has been located everywhere from its original home on Beatty Street to an abandoned Volkswagen garage to the old Watson glove factory on East 2nd—and looks forward to keeping the curtain raised for another 50 years.

Vancouver
604.873.3311 www.vancouverplayhouse.com

Top, The Miracle Worker, *Bridget O'Sullivan, Jennifer Clement, Margot Berner, and Anna Cummer; center left,* The Drowsy Chaperone, *Thom Allison and Gabrielle Jones; center right,* Toronto, Mississippi, *William McDonald; bottom,* Miss Julie: Freedom Summer, *Caroline Cave and Kevin Hanchard; photographs courtesy of David Cooper*

VAN DOP GALLERY

British Columbia's premier contemporary fine art and craft gallery, Van Dop Gallery features the inspiring work of skilled Canadian artisans. Since 1996 Trudy Van Dop has delighted visitors with her handpicked collection representing some of the most imaginative contemporary artists of our time.

A visit to the gallery is a cultural experience. The space showcases high-quality hand-blown and sculptured glass, distinctive porcelain and ceramic pieces, hand-forged metal sculptures, original paintings, and hand-turned wood bowls. Trudy is passionate about understanding the artists' stories and the symbolism behind each piece; she loves to share her knowledge with guests, especially those new to Canadian arts and crafts. As a highly recognized fine art consultant, she will meet one-on-one with art lovers to select the perfect piece or commission an exclusive work. Trudy holds a philosophy about the joy of giving and receiving: "When you have an emotional connection with an artist's work, the piece will touch others in the same way." Presenting a gift of art impresses the recipient and always rewards the giver. And from art delivery and installation to personal and corporate gifts with custom engraving and gift wrapping, Trudy's art of service is unsurpassed.

421 Richmond Street, New Westminster
888.981.9886 www.vandopgallery.com

Photographs by Emily Axness

Inn At The Quay, page 158

The Fairmont Waterfront, page 154

Pan Pacific Vancouver, page 162

Cathedral Mountain Lodge, page 172

Moda Hotel, page 161

Loden Vancouver Hotel, page 159

Pan Pacific Vancouver, page 162

The Westin Bayshore, Vancouver, page 168

RELAX

HOTELS & SPAS

Unwind. Repose. Let go. Hotels and spas offer relaxation in style, whether guests are reclining on plush beds or warm massage tables. Well-appointed luxury and boutique hotels, bed-and-breakfasts, resorts, spas, and salons make for the perfect vacation—or destination. Whether unwinding with an expert beauty service or getting comfortable amid luxurious hospitality amenities, the right reservation can be the most memorable component of a British Columbia sojourn.

ABIGAIL'S HOTEL

A Tudor-inspired bed-and-breakfast in the heart of Victoria that regularly draws international guests is a gem in Vancouver Island's crown. Abigail's Hotel is a picturesque boutique hotel—neatly tucked into a cul-de-sac and surrounded by English gardens—offering the comfort of a family home with convenient access to the capital's attractions. Guests can enjoy elegantly appointed rooms, homemade breakfasts, and a convivial ambience while taking advantage of the delightfully mild climate, various architectural landmarks, eclectic arts scene, and diverse landscape.

The hotel's owner, Ellen Cmolik, purchased Abigail's in 2003 after falling in love with the charming city while visiting her son at university. A retired accountant residing in Vancouver, Ellen found that running a bed-and-breakfast would fulfill her mutual desires to work and to regularly visit one of her favorite destinations. Alongside her well-trained staff, Ellen welcomes locals looking for a change of pace as well as visitors from around the globe. Tourists from the likes of England, Italy, and Japan are drawn to Abigail's for its cozy, communal atmosphere that provides people the chance to reconnect with themselves, with their spouses, and with others.

The enchanting setting at Abigail's makes it an ideal locale for intimate weddings and receptions. And the hotel's reputation for excellence in amenities and service clearly precedes it, on an international scale. Indeed, a Japanese couple flew themselves and their wedding party from Japan to get married at Abigail's, filling all of the hotel's 23 rooms and requiring an interpreter to communicate with the staff. Adding to the already ample amenities are designated pet-friendly rooms, with leashes and crates available at the front desk. As the perennial temperate conditions render the destination always "in season," Abigail's Hotel boasts an abundance of guests year-round.

906 McClure Street, Victoria
800.561.6565 www.abigailshotel.com

Photographs: top by Randal Kurt; bottom and right by Rob Destrube

April Point Resort & Spa

Dreaming of an idyllic place where you can escape to nature, share an adventure, or simply renew your senses? Beautiful Quadra Island's April Point Resort & Spa fits that bill. The unique coastal paradise is a historic property where breathtaking scenery, vibrant marine life, and the relaxed pace of the islands come together to create an unforgettable vacation.

Nestled in Discovery Passage, this area is known as "The Heart of the Pacific Playground" for good reason. From lively salmon fishing and kayaking to wilderness hiking, there's no shortage of incredible experiences. Picturesque tours of Quadra Island abound by seaplane, helicopter, bicycle, and motor scooter. Open from May through September, April Point has a sister resort, Painter's Lodge, linked by water shuttle. Guests may stay at either and enjoy the activities of both.

At the end of a fun-filled day, the resort's oceanfront Aveda spa encourages guests to rejuvenate in a serene Japanese-inspired retreat. Ocean-view accommodations—from cabins to luxury suites—prioritize comfort and feature rustic elegance décor, a nod to the site's origins as an angler's lodge in the 1940s. Today, April Point is a coveted island getaway that showcases stunning scenery and wondrous wildlife.

900 April Point Road, Quathiaski Cove
250.285.2222 www.aprilpoint.com

Photographs courtesy of April Point Resort & Spa

Hotel Grand Pacific

The Hotel Grand Pacific is a savvy traveler's dream come true, especially after receiving the prestigious Four Diamond award as a full-service hotel and the *Wine Spectator* award for an impressive wine list in The Mark. Situated in the heart of Victoria on the beautiful Inner Harbour with the Olympic Mountains nearby, readers of *Condé Nast* voted it the Best Hotel in Canada in 2008. But accolades aside, go see for yourself—modern luxury and warm West Coast hospitality embrace you upon arrival. An extraordinary staff is at your beck and call for a highly personalized experience, whether here for a leisure trip or on corporate business.

Amenities abound. Elegant rooms and suites have feng shui décor and airy private balconies offering city and waterfront views. The Spa at the Grand's aesthetic services and relaxing body-mind treatments support your wellbeing, while The Grand Pacific Athletic Club features a 25-meter pool, hydrotherapy tub, and exercise equipment for a fitness boost after a British brewpub crawl downtown. Dining is pure heaven at The Mark, with its West Coast fusion cuisine and international thousand-bottle wine cellar sure to sate the connoisseur's palate. Guests are privy to everything Victoria has to offer while staying at the Hotel Grand Pacific with art galleries, cultural spots, lively cafés, and seasonal festivals only steps away. Whether appreciating the architectural splendor of the Parliament Buildings or playing a round of golf with a majestic mountain backdrop, the Hotel Grand Pacific is a world-class destination worthy of a fascinating new entry in anyone's travel journal.

463 Belleville Street, Victoria
800.663.7550 www.hotelgrandpacific.com

Photographs by Rich Farr

ALL ABOUT YOU SPA RETREAT

Where beauty and rest converge—that's the philosophy behind All About You Spa Retreat, a modern hideaway that combines all the comforts of a bed-and-breakfast with a full menu of therapeutic spa treatments available steps from your room. The space even doubles as a venue for exclusive private spa parties where celebrities can steal away from the prying eyes of the paparazzi.

Long familiar with aesthetics as a former model and cosmetology school vice president, founder and owner Raylene Walker opened up her home as a B&B spa retreat in 2009 after moving from her spa she had run in Vancouver's English Bay for more than a decade. All About You specializes in health and recovery programs led by a naturopathic doctor and carried out in a relaxing retreat atmosphere, and the range of spa treatments offered is extensive.

Located in Lions Bay, a small artsy community near West Vancouver on the way to Whistler, Raylene's elegant entertainment home with its open, airy floorplan and modern design features two bedrooms in a full private suite that offer all the accoutrements of fine lodging. With your own personal beach right outside your door and the house's creekside location, spectacular water views make it easy to feel like you've escaped the hustle and bustle, and access to hiking, golf, skiing, shopping, and dining are just minutes away.

15 Oceanview Road, Lions Bay
604.682.7716 www.allaboutyouspagroup.com

Photographs courtesy of Fotolia.com

Aquae Sulis Holistic Spa

Be transported from the busy shopping square into a peaceful, inviting, and warm Moroccan-style atmosphere at the Aquae Sulis Holistic Spa, where relaxation and natural elements take precedence. The rejuvenating atmosphere begins in a comfortable reception room with a hot cup of organic loose leaf tea. A private relaxation room can further enhance the soul.

Instead of focusing on outer beauty, the spa recognizes that inner beauty and feeling good are of ultimate importance. Its balanced approach to beauty and health relies on ancient healing rituals and beauty treatments using high-quality products that are exempt of chemical ingredients. All therapies are performed by hand, with not a steamer or other machine in sight.

Guests may choose from chemical-free treatments inspired by Hawaii, Africa, India, Shangri-La, and the Dead Sea, or from the generous spa menu of massages, manicures, pedicures, and hair removal procedures. There are also Dr. Hauschka brand facials and facial rejuvenation treatments by Dr. Harjot Parmer, natural health doctor and spa owner. These processes are designed to work with the skin and body's natural methods of healing and restoration in a luxurious, pampering experience.

100-1169 56th Street, Delta
604.943.3560 www.aquaesulis-spa.com

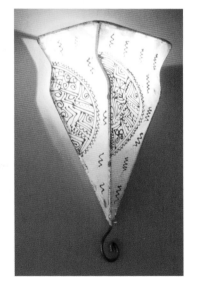

Photographs by Jullian Price

BRITISH COLUMBIA HOTEL ASSOCIATION

The British Columbia Hotel Association was established during Prohibition, 1917, to build hotels—the only way to legally serve alcohol. In the mid-'80s, the association shifted its focus from room and beverages to travel and tourism. It was Grace McCarthy, a government minister, who fostered this shift in thinking and whose big-picture focus helped to coordinate the association's new mandate in time for Expo '86.

In a similar fashion, Vancouver's 2010 Olympic and Paralympic Winter Games allowed the association to concentrate on showing the 3 billion spectators—most of whom had never visited Canada—a world-class city with fabulous facilities.

Over the past 30 years the association has grown to become a strong resource and advocate for the hotel industry in the province. With members and associates from across the region, the association is dedicated to improving and strengthening the growing tourism and hospitality industry. The association works diligently to keep hotel standards at the highest possible position by elevating the quality of staff training and, overall, the standards of this service-oriented sector.

Choose from many popular destinations: enjoy a rustic beachfront location at Tofino's Wickaninnish Inn, gaze out onto Vancouver's Lions Gate Bridge, or survey the harbor from Victoria's majestic The Fairmont Empress.

200-948 Howe Street, Vancouver

Photographs: left by Tom Ryan; right courtesy of Tourism British Columbia

CHERRY BLOSSOM BED AND BREAKFAST

What do you do when you suddenly find yourself empty-nesters in a home much too large for just two, but one that holds three generations of family history? The only common-sense thing to do: Open your home as a bed-and-breakfast and offer guests five-star service at a reasonable rate and with more love than anyone else can.

That's the philosophy behind Cherry Blossom Bed and Breakfast. "We enjoy sharing our home, our heritage, and our hearts with people," says hostess Alison Bentall, who owns the home with her husband David. "This is a 'real home' located in an exclusive and elegant neighborhood."

Every morning visitors are treated to a gourmet breakfast—served in the home's dining room or at a table for two overlooking the gardens—while fresh-baked cookies are part of the personal service that is offered to every guest throughout the afternoon. The French Provincial-style home has extensive private gardens, a swimming pool and hot tub, and a lovely vine-covered cherry tree. The interiors are stylish yet relaxing with inlaid hardwood floors and Persian carpets. Guests may choose from two finely appointed one-bedroom suites and a two-bedroom family-friendly suite.

The home, located near the grounds of the annual Cherry Blossom Festival, is only a short drive from downtown Vancouver and just a 10-minute walk from the charming Kerrisdale shopping district.

2610 West 50th Avenue, Vancouver
877.290.4368 www.cherryblossombb.com

Photographs by Catriana van Rijn

151

il Destino Salon & Spa

A rare combination of refined style and serenity awaits at il Destino Salon & Spa. Entering through the elegant, ebonized double doors framed by a vibrant red brick façade is like stepping into another world.

The creative vision of Laura Mah, this exclusive full-service salon and day spa treats guests with the personalized attention only offered in the most renowned private retreats. Passionate about her Italian heritage, Laura brought years of experience from the elite beauty industry to Port Moody, opening the doors of il Destino in 2006. The salon's moniker—translating to "destiny"—was inspired by her father's wise philosophy: "If it is meant to happen, it will." Laura, along with a talented and impressively credentialed staff, is committed to bringing every guest a sense of comfort and peace, echoing the natural beauty that surrounds the salon. Hair designs, pedicures, facials, spa treatments, and all forms of pampering are on the menu, ready to be enjoyed. And as evidenced by her heartfelt support of charitable causes, Laura has a generous spirit that extends beyond the walls of the spa.

2610 St. Johns Street, Port Moody
604.939.2610 www.ildestino.com

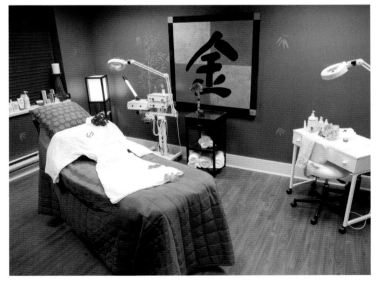

Photographs by Keith Mah

THE FAIRMONT WATERFRONT

The Fairmont Waterfront takes a natural perspective on business and pleasure. This isn't just about amenities. As a gateway to Asia and the Pacific Rim, the hotel combines Eastern and Western philosophies right in the heart of Vancouver, so that those who want to experience the unique beauty of this city are enveloped with honesty and integrity. Connected to the Vancouver Convention Centre, The Fairmont Waterfront is an amalgamation of shopping, dining, and sightseeing in one distinctive package. And it's now the green standard in the industry.

It's the duality that makes it so intriguing. On the roof deck, you look one way and it's natural splendor—mountains and Burrard Inlet; look the other, you get the cosmopolitan downtown. The Fairmont has also turned that roof into a green landscape, where an organic garden grows the restaurant's fruits and vegetables, and where maintained bees thrive. Being innovative with its ideas and focusing on doing the right thing at all levels, The Fairmont Waterfront defines a culture strong in spirit, giving back to the environment in sustainability and as a clear presence in Vancouver's skyline.

900 Canada Place Way, Vancouver
604.691.1991 www.fairmont.com/waterfront

Photographs courtesy of The Fairmont Waterfront

FLAMING JUNE DAY SPA

Named after an 1895 Frederick Leighton painting imbued with luxury and peace, Flaming June Day Spa has been transformed into a haven of comfort and beauty befitting its namesake by owners Mike and Debby Weber, who have run the business since 2004. With the motto of nourishing the mind, body, and soul, the Webers have created a professional but unpretentious experience that allows all who walk through the doors to truly treat themselves.

Just through the door, whimsical murals line the walls of the main spa area to exude a soothing Mediterranean atmosphere. Guests can be pampered with a variety of treatments, ranging from mini to advanced facials to refreshing manicures and pedicures and full body treatments like the revitalizing glacial clay and Pacific seaweed wrap. Services are performed using leading brand name beauty and skincare products.

In the standalone, century-old Spa Cottage, couples or groups of up to 10 can relax or celebrate in exotic South Pacific style. The seclusion from other guests allows intimate and customized festivities to occur during the luxurious services—guests are invited to bring their favorite refreshments, music, and anything else to enhance the spa occasion.

1701 Grant Street, Vancouver
604.253.8001 www.flamingjune.com

Photographs by Sheri Frailick

156

HADDON HOUSE BED & BREAKFAST

Just steps from Deer Lake Park, with its pristine lake and native trails, a quiet, genteel neighborhood houses Haddon House Bed & Breakfast. Set within a glorious confusion of flowers, butterflies, and birds, the house speaks to grander times. Haddon House is what bed-and-breakfasts are supposed to be: Old World charm in a tranquil oasis. In 2007, Johannes and Marie-Louise Stolz renovated and refurbished this 1923 home to its original splendor, winning a B.C. Heritage Association award for authenticity.

Haddon House is a step back in time, but with modern conveniences cleverly blending in. The foyer is gracious, the rooms elegant—guests can even have breakfast on a sweeping deck that overlooks luscious gardens.

This heritage building is exquisitely furnished, with a grand piano that graces hardwood floors, and with comfortable chairs and couches that invite you to stop and rest a while. The Stolzes are often instant friends with their guests because of the personal nature of their establishment. In fact, when you first arrive, you are received by a beautiful lady with a gentle nature, a big smile, and liquid brown eyes, and that's just Duchess, the golden lab retriever, the true host of Haddon House Bed & Breakfast.

5558 Buckingham Avenue, Burnaby
888.522.2363 www.haddonhouse.ca

Photographs by Mathias Fast

Inn At The Quay

Intimate. Luxe. Riverfront. Just 30 minutes by SkyTrain from Vancouver on the mighty Fraser River sits Inn At The Quay, New Westminster's decidedly boutique and über-chic hotel. New Westminster is a fabulous mix of old and new, with picturesque waterfront walkways and beautiful Victorian architecture, making your stay at the inn quite the enriching experience. Stroll the two-mile stretch and watch freighters and tugs ply the busy waters, or catch a paddlewheeler riverboat tour right from the Inn's dock. At the foot of the hotel discover the Boathouse Restaurant which serves up an extensive seafood menu, with excellent service and waterside views, or follow the boardwalk to the River Market at Westminster Quay and fascinating Fraser River Discovery Centre.

Whether arriving for a romantic weekend or extended business trip, the finely appointed hotel interiors will capture your senses. Guestrooms have a contemporary, couture feeling with textural fabrics and vivid schemes

of marine blue, refreshing aqua, and brilliant fuchsia. Unexpected custom art headboards plus stylish linens provide a luxuriously sophisticated ambience. And relaxing with friends in the stylish living room lobby has never been more inviting, with cheeky chairs and sofas that clearly exhibit South Beach soul. After a long day out and about, slip into a plush robe and step into a spa-inspired private bath. Reserve your favorite vintage during swanky wine flight nights, or sip some bubbly on champagne Saturdays. It's fair to say that Inn At The Quay is the place to be for a much needed jaunt, planned vacation, or any festive occasion, from family wedding celebrations to energizing corporate retreats.

900 Quayside Drive, New Westminster
604.520.1776 www.innatthequay.com

Photographs courtesy of Inn At The Quay

LODEN VANCOUVER HOTEL

Loden Vancouver sparkles at the edge of Coal Harbour, downtown Vancouver's premiere luxury neighborhood. The hotel's 77 stylish guestrooms and one-bedroom suites—plus an expansive two-bedroom penthouse christened the Halo—are encased in an exterior of curved glass, natural stone, and copper, mimicking the waves of the nearby waterfront. Floor-to-ceiling windows and sliding interior walls allow not only an abundance of natural light, but also provide breathtaking views of Stanley Park and the bustling downtown business district.

Inside, a modern aesthetic and sophisticated palette of caramel, coral, and chocolate brown translate into the ultimate boutique hotel experience. Since opening in late 2008, Loden has welcomed business and leisure travelers with its cosmopolitan charm and immaculate attention to detail. Such creature comforts as step-out patios, heated tiles in the bathrooms, and complimentary downtown car service heighten the experience.

Executive chef Marc-Andre Choquette helms Voya, Loden's lobby-level intimate 80-seat restaurant and lounge. Voya abandons the familiar with its globally inspired cuisine. Inventive, internationally fused dishes feature fresh, local, and organic ingredients, always true to the season. Soak up the retro-glamour atmosphere and the sumptuous setting: Icy white lacquer tables, decadent chocolate banquettes, timeless blue upholstery, and towering mirrors catch the glow from glimmering chandeliers. Give in to a midday cocktail, gear down after work, or get set to spin late at night. The sleek sophistication melds perfectly with the chic Vancouver surroundings.

1177 Melville Street, Vancouver
604.669.5060 www.theloden.com

Photographs courtesy of Loden Vancouver Hotel

MINT HAIR LOUNGE

Not your typical quiet salon, Mint Hair Lounge is an intimate, funky boutique bustling with activity. Step out of Port Moody into a vibrant atmosphere where strangers immediately become friends and feel at home. With a focus on modern, fashion-forward thinking, Lisa Robinson and her team ensure each guest can sit back, have a good time, and then leave feeling refreshed and energized.

Whether your ideal cut is a classy style or a more trendy look, and whether you're looking to enhance your natural color or try something new, the stylists can get the job done—just with more passion and creativity than the average salon. Selected for their flair and expertise, the talented stylists tap into their competitive nature and delve into the hair industry to fully take advantage of everything available. From a fantastic style in the salon to photo shoots, hair shows, or community projects, every aspect is accomplished with an excitement and dedication that is second to none.

2337 Clarke Street, Port Moody
604.936.3661 www.minthairlounge.com

Photographs: top left and bottom third by Bluelava Studio; top right, bottom left, bottom second, and bottom right by Dana Smith Photography

MODA HOTEL

In the vibrant heart of downtown Vancouver's arts and cultural district, Moda Hotel serves as not only a unique 57-room boutique hotel but also an elegant testimonial to the city's rich social and artistic past. Built and opened in 1908, the hotel possesses its original Old World architecture while boasting modern, contemporary interior design and technology. Such authentic touches as 100-year-old exposed mosaic tile floors in the lobby and bathrooms and 80-year-old hardwood flooring in select rooms and on the stairs retain the building's heritage.

More than just a hotel, the property is the sum of all its unique and lavish aspects. A connoisseur of the finest in dining and spirits need not travel far beyond the lobby. Uva Wine Bar and Cibo Trattoria present patrons with Italian-inspired cuisine, including the best wine pairings and freshest local ingredients that Vancouver's culinary scene has to offer. Business services for executives and designated rooms for animal lovers are just a few of the features available to the discerning traveler seeking both modern comforts and a sense of history.

900 Seymour Street, Vancouver
604.683.4251 www.modahotel.ca

Photographs: top and bottom by Raef Grohne; center by Derek Lepper

Pan Pacific Vancouver

Instantly recognizable for stunning architecture and famed for service and culinary achievement, the Pan Pacific Vancouver offers incomparable views and immediate access to the mountains, harbor, Stanley Park, and the magnificent city skyline. Located atop a pier that overlooks the city's breathtaking waterfront, the hotel and its numerous amenities serve guests who expect the finest in luxury and comfort.

With reverence and dedication to the community, the hotel sponsors hundreds of local organizations and hosts charities, fundraisers, and galas. A part of the Green Key Eco-Rating Program, the Pan Pacific Vancouver team is committed to alleviating environmental impact by upholding the highest green measures of energy conservation, water conservation, and solid waste management.

Celebrated for exquisite culinary artistry, the hotel's several waterfront restaurants provide an award-winning selection of mouthwatering West Coast cuisine, and its Spa Utopia is a soothing retreat offering the best

in relaxation and rejuvenation. Just minutes from historic Gastown, the Robson Street boutiques, and the 200-shop Pacific Centre Mall—and steps away from the city's spectacular cruise ship terminal—the Pan Pacific Vancouver stands as a testament to the loftiest standards of accommodation.

999 Canada Place, Vancouver
604.662.8111 www.panpacific.com/vancouver

Photographs courtesy of Pan Pacific Vancouver

TRIUMF House

Originally established to serve the scientists performing research at TRIUMF, Canada's National Laboratory for Particle and Nuclear Physics, TRIUMF House is located on the breathtakingly scenic University of British Columbia campus. Frequented by those who relish a quiet, comfortable atmosphere at affordable prices, the guest house is within easy access to the trails of Pacific Spirit Park and the university's Nitobe Memorial Garden, Thunderbird Winter Sports Centre, and The Chan Centre for the Performing Arts, as well as downtown Vancouver and Vancouver International Airport—even Stanley Park. Guests may also take the opportunity to tour TRIUMF and see the many facilities that have made it one of the preeminent laboratories in the world.

Inside the house, a lounge with fireplace and piano presents opportunities for warm relaxing evenings while the fully equipped commercial kitchen provides the tools and workspace to accommodate guests' culinary adventures. Easily accessible by all, the facilities also include a computer room, workout room, and secure underground parking as well as such services as bike rental and a guest laundry room.

Whether hosting travelers or visiting scholars, TRIUMF House is the perfect home away from home. At TRIUMF House, guests come first, and the friendly and helpful staff's mission is to thoroughly understand the needs of the guests and consistently surpass their expectations by delivering personal and intuitive service.

5835 Thunderbird Boulevard, Vancouver
604.222.7633 www.triumfhouse.ca

Photographs by Shirley Reeve

THE WESTIN BAYSHORE, VANCOUVER

A journey worthy of travelogue notes begins at The Westin Bayshore, Vancouver. Built in 1961, the landmark hotel offers guests the best of both worlds: Vancouver's cultural activities and a relaxing resort experience. This unique combination of features landed The Westin Bayshore a coveted spot on *Condé Nast Traveler*'s Gold List a few years ago.

Boasting its own convention center and the largest hotel ballroom in Western Canada, the hotel plays host to weddings, corporate functions, and star-studded events. Guests are instantly enamored by breathtaking views of the coastline, distant mountains, and Stanley Park's urban forest with ancient trees. Beyond its natural surroundings, the resort property has earned high marks from the Green Key eco-rating program for environmental stewardship.

The Westin Bayshore enjoys a beautiful waterfront location in historic Coal Harbour and takes advantage of its ocean setting with a private marina. Business and convention travelers, families, and international vacationers find tranquility in the sprawling seven-acre property with amenities around every corner, and the thriving, vibrant downtown epicenter offering urban sophistication is just steps away.

Accommodations include heavenly white linen-dressed beds and lavish baths designed with Westin's signature comfort and luxury expressed in every detail. Fitness is also a priority at The Westin Bayshore, which has indoor and outdoor pools and a fitness center to keep everyone energized. Special guestrooms with a built-in treadmill and exercise equipment are even available. Cruiser bicycles are available for landlubbers, while a pleasure floatplane, yacht charters, and whale watching await visiting sea lovers.

1601 Bayshore Drive, Vancouver
604.682.3377 www.westinbayshore.com

Photographs courtesy of The Westin Bayshore, Vancouver

PRESTIGE HOTELS & RESORTS

Prestige Hotels & Resorts has come a long way from its humble beginnings in 1963 when Josef Huber Sr. and his wife Anna purchased one modest motel in Penticton. Joined by Joe Huber Jr. in 1985, Prestige Hotels & Resorts' portfolio has grown to its present-day status consisting of 10 family-owned and operated premier properties offering world-class accommodation and superior service.

Located in the Okanagan, Kootenay Rockies, and on Vancouver Island, each smoke-free hotel or resort offers the opportunity for a truly unique regional experience. Whether you are in the mood to sample local delicacies, stroll through an idyllic town, relax in revitalizing hot springs, ski pristine slopes, or tee off on an immaculate golf course, there is a Prestige Hotels & Resorts destination for you. Locations include Kelowna, Vernon, Salmon Arm, Golden, Radium, Cranbrook, Nelson, and Rossland. The most recent addition to the chain is The Prestige Oceanfront Resort & Convention Centre located on Vancouver Island in Sooke, a stunning seaside town situated between majestic old growth forests and the awe-inspiring beaches of the Pacific Ocean coast.

In each community where a hotel or resort has been developed, the company has earned the reputation of being the leading provider of accommodations, a corporation with honest core values and devoted employees who are proud to represent their employer. With a firm understanding of the past, a nod to tradition, and an eye on the future, Prestige Hotels & Resorts invites visitors to enjoy the very best of British Columbia while their expert staff caters to every need to make each visit a truly remarkable experience.

516 Lawrence Avenue, Kelowna
877.737.8443 www.PrestigeHotelsAndResorts.com

Photographs courtesy of Prestige Hotels and Resorts

SCANDINAVE SPA WHISTLER

For centuries, aching bodies have found relief with the Finnish bathing tradition now known as hydrotherapy or Scandinavian baths. The alternation of warm baths, a cold rinse, and a period of relaxation—all in the heart of nature—produces a deep sense of wellbeing, soothing and cleansing mind, body, and spirit. Denizens of Whistler have an opportunity to experience this age-old process for themselves at Scandinave Spa, the fourth such outpost of the Scandinave spa group.

While following in the footsteps of its sister spas, the Whistler iteration—the first in Western Canada—is the largest and greenest in the portfolio so far, enabling an eco-friendly experience that will assuage your conscience as well as your muscles. Innovations like reusable bags, stainless steel water bottles, staff uniforms made of sustainable fibers, passive solar heating, a high-efficiency furnace, and vegetated green roofs all help the complex minimize its impact on the environment.

Etched into a hillside of spruce and cedar, the nature-immersive spa overlooks a mountain and borders bike trails and parks. Spanning 20,000 square feet across six buildings and integrated with three acres of forest, the Nordic-style all-season spa is meant to harmonize with its setting as guided by principles of sustainability. Indoor and outdoor facilities include a eucalyptus steam bath, a wood-burning Finnish sauna, hot and cold baths, Nordic and thermal waterfalls, solariums, terraces, an outdoor fireplace, and hammocks.

Whether you're a local, visiting Whistler for a day or night, or spending the season, you'll benefit from the unbelievably unique amenities offered by Scandinave Spa.

8010 Mons Road, Whistler
604.935.2424 www.scandinave.com

Photographs: above and facing page left by Gregory J. Eymundson; facing page top by Elissa Mulligan-Gauvreau; facing page center and bottom by Todd Lawson

CATHEDRAL MOUNTAIN LODGE

When the busy world begins to catch up with you, there's no better place on earth to relax, regroup, and replenish than Cathedral Mountain Lodge, nestled in an enclave amid the glacier-peaked Canadian Rockies. Imagine staying in luxurious, secluded log cabins with the inviting touches of your favorite fine hotel: cozy wood-burning fireplaces, fluffy down duvets, and freshly brewed coffee. Gazing out lodge windows brings awe-inspiring nature into view, revealing majestic pines and the pristine Kicking Horse River.

Outdoor buffs step right outside their doors to enjoy miles of hiking and horseback-riding trails, alpine meadows, canoeing adventures, and the abundant flora and fauna of historic Yoho National Park. Some may say it's heaven on earth—and entries in the lodge's guestbook express that very sentiment time and time again. Luxury appointments abound to meet every wish for comfort, but the hideaway promises no televisions or cell phones to disturb peaceful getaways. Cathedral Mountain Lodge assures an unforgettable experience through its culinary offerings sure to satisfy a hearty appetite after mountain excursions, a cozy fireside great room for conviviality, and epic waterfalls nearby that clearly enliven the soul. Whether seeking alone time for quiet contemplation, photographic opportunities, or exhilarating outdoor activities, an escape to Cathedral Mountain Lodge will generously bestow enough fond memories to last a lifetime.

Yoho Valley Road, Field
866.619.6442 www.cathedralmountain.com

Photographs: left by Capilano Group of Companies; facing page courtesy of Cathedral Mountain Lodge

Milano Boutique Coffee Roasters, page 195

Sumac Ridge Estate Winery, page 201

The Marina Restaurant, page 194

NK'Mip Cellars, page 199

Spinnakers Gastro Brewpub & Guesthouses, page 177

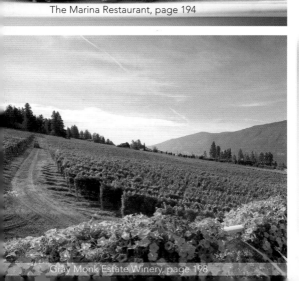
Gray Monk Estate Winery, page 198

Cactus Club Cafe, page 181

Into Chocolate Specialty Sweets, page 191

INDULGE

RESTAURANTS & LOUNGES

Taste. Sip. Savor. Delicious restaurants and eateries populate every street and town in the province, and a myriad of different types means visitors and locals are perpetually tempted to indulge. In addition to bistros, coffee shops, cafés, teahouses, bakeries, and chocolatiers, there are nightclubs, bars, lounges, and even wineries and breweries. From casual dining to upscale environments to delectable sweetshops and coffeehouses, each type of atmosphere is bound to have a dish or libation to satisfy even the fussiest of palates.

SPINNAKERS GASTRO BREWPUB & GUESTHOUSES

In the early 1980s, architect and beer aficionado Paul Hadfield experienced a eureka moment. Partner and Canadian craft-brewing pioneer John Mitchell had brought back a collection of English beers from the United Kingdom. Inspired by these, Paul, John, and a third partner determined that British Columbia needed access to a wider range of beers with flavor—and set about creating what was to become the first purpose-built Canadian brewpub of the modern era. With generous assistance from disaffected commercial brewers and local homebrewers, the intrepid team aimed to produce beers that would be on par with some of the best in the world. After 18 months of dogged persistence involving nothing less than changing civic bylaws, provincial liquor laws, and the Canadian Federal Excise Act, Spinnakers Gastro Brewpub was born.

With a purpose of enhancing the local area, Spinnakers first created a fantastic homebrew using the best technology available and then set out to discover and foster artisan growers and producers of exceptional regional food. Both have been achieved. As the oldest Canadian brewpub, Spinnakers' brewers craft ales, lagers, and seasonal specialty beers using only the finest ingredients, pure aquifer water, and time-honored Old World brewing techniques. In addition to its amazing beverages, the brewpub serves up fresh, seasonal fare, all prepared from scratch on the premises with local, seasonal, and sustainable ingredients. From beer-based artisan breads to house-smoked wild seafood, Spinnakers defines the art of the Gastro Brewpub, which simply means "gastronomically amazing fare."

Guests are encouraged to stop by for a drink, stick around for dinner, come back for lunch the next day, browse the deli, bakery, and chocolate creations at Provisions, and stay at one of the elegant guesthouses located steps from the brewpub. Hailed as Victoria's gathering place, Spinnakers sums up the best the city has to offer, with stunning views and world-class fare that can only be found on southern Vancouver Island.

308 Catherine Street, Victoria
250.386.2739 www.spinnakers.com

Photographs by Gary McKinstry

THE BEACH HOUSE RESTAURANT & LOUNGE

Delicious food. Friendly atmosphere. Amazing views. What more could you want in a place to enjoy a nice dinner, relaxing lunch, or special occasion? At The Beach House Restaurant & Lounge, guests receive all three essentials for a wonderful meal. With a focus on the idea that simplicity does not translate to a lack of sophistication, the establishment has received numerous awards, including *Vancouver Magazine*'s best North Shore restaurant award.

Situated at the foot of West Vancouver's Dundarave Pier in a restored 1912 historic teahouse, The Beach House boasts a bustling lounge, sophisticated dining room, heated beachside patio, and private terraced room that all overlook Burrard Inlet and Stanley Park. Monthly wine events offer locals and visitors alike the opportunity to participate in tastings, hobnob with renowned vintners, and refresh their taste buds.

In an effort to become eco-friendly, The Beach House has committed to the Ocean Wise program, which strives to keep ocean life healthy and abundant for years to come. To delight the most refined palates, the chefs use only the freshest, finest ingredients available—locally sourced when possible—to create seasonally inspired dishes paired with perfectly matched wines.

150-25 Street, West Vancouver
604.922.1414 www.thebeachhouserestaurant.ca

Photograph by Shawn Hallgren

THE BEDFORD HOUSE RESTAURANT & LOUNGE

As a perfect end to a day filled with the hustle and bustle of Vancouver or the many sightseeing opportunities throughout British Columbia, locals and visitors alike enjoy an upscale restaurant with international style at The Bedford House, located in the quaint, historic Fort Langley village along the Fraser River.

Originally known as The Haldi House, the impressive structure was built in 1904 by Jacob Haldi and his wife, Jessie, through a large inheritance from Jessie's father. Until 1975, the house remained a private residence, at which point Austrian chef and businessman Herb Feischl refurbished the building—while still maintaining the original character of the house and its stately grounds—and opened the restaurant. Since then, The Bedford House has become a local tradition for everything from special occasions to casual meals.

The Austrian-trained chef and a dedicated staff ensure a friendly, attentive, and unpretentious fine dining experience. The European-inspired menu, which is based on locally sourced food, and the rooms' country-elegant aesthetic establish a relaxed feeling that guests will enjoy on any occasion.

9272 Glover Road, Fort Langley
604.888.2333 www.fortlangleyvillage.com

Photographs by Jason Hughes

179

BOMBAY BHEL

If you're familiar with Indian food, you'll know that "bhel" is a kind of snack: roasted puffed rice, tamarind chutney, onions, potatoes, and chickpeas, served cold. Twenty years ago, Bombay Bhel began in Toronto as a hub of Indian takeout snacks, or "chaats." Now, the restaurant has expanded, and people from all over flock to its remarkable delicacies, including its most popular dish, buttered chicken: tender pieces of tandoori chicken simmered in a velvety sauce made from butter, tomatoes, and cream. This is northern Indian food with a North American twist.

Bombay Bhel is the community's restaurant, not some franchise machine. The owners' love of the community has given the restaurant an atmosphere of family, where everyone is greeted like an old friend—most of them now are, in fact. The restaurant seems at home when diners stay and talk, enjoying good food and good company. The décor is clean and uncluttered—pretentiousness is nowhere to be found. This simple, Old World philosophy of serving the community translates to Bombay Bhel's long-term, loyal, caring staff, who are a strong part of the family. As Bombay Bhel expands across British Columbia, it keeps its roots as a traditional restaurant. And having a mouthwatering menu makes it even better.

4266 East Hastings Street, Burnaby
604.299.2500 www.bombaybhelrestaurant.com

Photograph by Meghan Jones

CACTUS CLUB CAFE

An exquisite culinary experience should reflect the personality of its region, and the Cactus Club Cafe offers its guests the fusion of fine dining in an upscale yet casual atmosphere. Each location boasts a unique personality, replete with an original art collection and a first-class team made up of energetic, ambitious, intelligent, and friendly people who are trained in all aspects of professional culinary service. The unique collection consistently has the largest number of apprenticing chefs in Western Canada, who are developed and guided to achieve their chef accreditation under the leadership and direction of Rob Feenie, Canada's only "Iron Chef" champion.

Hailing from humble beginnings, the ever-expanding and growing Cactus Club Cafe is now comprised of 20 restaurants within British Columbia and Alberta. Cactus Club's main focus is food, and each dish is crafted with the finest local ingredients available—local Ocean Wise-endorsed seafood, sashimi-grade tuna caught within 300 kilometers of the Vancouver coast, local artisan bread, and fresh berries in the summer. Cactus Club Cafe's award-winning wine list showcases the best of BC brands, and the cafe team works diligently to offer handcrafted, unique beverages, such as signature margaritas with hand-squeezed fresh limes for each drink. The staff members aim to make sophistication accessible, a state of continuous improvement that competitors try to duplicate but can never replicate.

588 Burrard Street, Vancouver
604.682.0933 www.cactusclubcafe.com

Photographs: top left by Clayton Perry; top center by Janet Rerecich, top right and bottom by Bruce Law

CENTRAL BISTRO

Nestled in downtown Vancouver as an integral part of its West End, Central Bistro is known as a neighborhood hangout with a loyal following of regulars from the local community, but visitors are more than welcome. Owned by a former Lamborghini mechanic who fell in love with Italian cooking, the casual bistro prepares scrumptious comfort food with a European flair, all made from scratch.

The funky, down-to-earth atmosphere of Central fits right in with the fun, urban feel of the West End. The food mimics that same style. Chef Ian adds his unique recipes to the mainstays of meat pies, pastas, and Irish soda bread. His philosophy: "Sometimes a simple thing can be a beautiful thing." Not in the mood for a heavy meal? Central Bistro is also the right place for the lighter fare of soups, salads, sandwiches, and small plates. Locals love Central for its extensive and eclectic brunch menu, and it's proven quite popular during the daytime on weekends.

In addition, special events are a highlight at the bistro. With a unique drink special or event practically every night of the week, each visitor finds something to enjoy. Guests can also hear live jazz every Sunday evening. Central's patio provides the perfect location to soak up the music and take in the fresh air.

1072 Denman Street, Vancouver
604.689.4527 www.centralbistro.com

Photographs: top left by Robert Stefanowicz; bottom left and right by Andre Larocque

CHRISTINE CATERING COMPANY, INC.

Taking her cue from Hollywood, Christine Irvine knew that if she built a catering company, the hungry would come. Indeed, they've been coming since 2003, when owner and chef Christine—a native of Alsace, France—began serving delectable goodies at everything from weddings to corporate luncheons as Christine Catering Company. She takes her company's motto, "We Cater to You," seriously; every menu is personalized to suit varying tastes and budgets, with absolutely no limits.

Aiding Christine in these culinary feats is her husband, Shean, plus more than 30 staff members. Each is carefully selected and trained to provide a welcoming, professional, and memorable experience. Also indispensable to Christine Catering is British Columbia itself. Local wine, vegetables, and salmon populate many of the menus, and Christine strives to make her meals with 80 percent Canadian products, most of which come from the province.

Besides being personally involved in every aspect of her company, Christine donates time and resources to numerous charities, including SHARE Society and Eagle Ridge Hospital Foundation. And every year Christine Catering provides the Port Moody Fire Department's annual Christmas tree chipping event with nutritious lunches, demonstrating that a business can be about more than the bottom line.

2821 Spring Street, Port Moody
604.461.6333 www.christinecatering.com

Photographs by Christine Irvine

THE CRAB SHOP

Known all over the Lower Mainland for its salmon, halibut, and cod fish and chips, North Vancouver's The Crab Shop is a favorite with locals and tourists alike. British Columbia native crooner Michael Bublé is a fan, as is movie star-turned-politician Arnold Schwarzenegger. Besides the award-winning fish and chips, the shop offers fresh fish, crab, shrimp, oysters, and lobster at competitive prices.

There are many ways to make a tasty crab cake, but most everyone will agree that loads of fresh Dungeness crab is what truly makes a winner. At The Crab Shop, an unassuming exterior belies the abundance of freshly caught and prepared seafood waiting inside. Every morning during the crab season, owner Marcel Gregori catches and processes the crab himself. Where else can you purchase crab cakes and meat from crabs caught and processed the same day?

In 2004 a sudden fire destroyed the original location, a dilapidated building opened in the 1960s that was periodically used by movie and television sets. The new location boasts a state-of-the-art kitchen and seafood display equipment, yet still offers the same high-quality take-out menu. It remains the perfect place to pick up picnic items for a family outing to Deep Cove, Cates Park, or almost any outdoor activity on the North Shore. Seafood fans have had no trouble following their taste buds to The Crab Shop's current location.

121-2455 Dollarton Highway, North Vancouver
604.929.1616

Photographs by Marcel Gregori

CRIME LAB

Before "CSI" there was Crime Lab, a Coal Harbour restaurant and late-night haunt. With floor-to-ceiling windows overlooking Coal Harbour Yacht Club, Crime Lab is a wonderful location for a fine dinner or drinks with friends.

The décor is West Coast modern with soft pendant lighting, dark wood tables and booths, and an outdoor patio that offers comfortable seating with incredible views. It's the perfect place to discuss past indiscretions while indulging in a few new ones over martinis.

Owner Kimberly Cole is a second-generation restaurateur who had been staking out this particular location for her restaurant for six years. When it became available, she was prepared to create an inviting setting that lives up to her motto of "Non-Members Only."

Crime Lab is well known for its menu of martinis—shaken or stirred—from the notorious 007 to Stab Wound, Exhibit A, Body Bag, DOA, and Crimes of Passion. A full menu for lunch and dinner offers everything from prime rib burgers to ahi tartare, saffron garlic prawns, and other delectable treats.

100-550 Denman Street, Vancouver
604.568.4606 www.crimelab.ca

Photography courtesy of Crime Lab

DONNELLY HOSPITALITY MANAGEMENT

With award-winning nightclubs, busy pubs, and a hugely popular cocktail lounge, Donnelly Hospitality Management has become the name of the game when it comes to exciting venues in the world-class city of Vancouver. Jeff Donnelly's vision and dedication transported London's modern pub culture here, changing the city's cocktail culture and nightlife scene. Today there are a number of DHM venues located within a five-minute walk of downtown: Bar None, The Lamplighter, Pop Opera, The Calling, Granville Room, Library Square, Republic, and The Modern, to name a few. Whether in English Bay, the charming Gastown district, or the club scene in the bustling Entertainment District, each stylish club, neighborhood bar, or pub has its own unique ambience.

DHM venues appeal to casual passersby and patrons who like to call ahead for celebrity treatment as well as party planners who value chic locations that have multimedia and street branding capabilities—not to mention mouthwatering cuisine prepared on-site. While impressive entertainment, modern designs, and attention to detail define the DHM family of venues, the company should also be noted for its impressive philanthropic efforts and encouragement of other local businesses to follow suit. The nonprofit Donnelly Fund is made possible through DHM's generous donation of 15 percent of its profits; the money goes straight to Vancouver families in need, which ultimately benefits the entire community.

Suite 302-1110 Hamilton Street, Vancouver
604.899.3229 www.dhmbars.ca

Photographs courtesy of Donnelly Hospitality Management

FLOATA SEAFOOD RESTAURANT

Where can you indulge in crispy Peking roasted duck, the iconic anatine dish originating from Beijing that's now the most famous entrée on Chinese menus? Prepared since the imperial era, it's now considered one of China's national foods and an international delicacy. Do you dream of a weekend dim sum brunch featuring 70 authentic Chinese delights? Look no further than historic Chinatown's brilliant pearl: Floata Seafood Restaurant.

For an authentic Chinese gastronomic experience, the downtown Vancouver restaurant is the choice of discerning dignitaries, conventioneers, and dining enthusiasts who have a taste for the traditional foods of Hong Kong. It has hosted the leading party of China and entertained Canadian prime ministers, Vancouver mayors, and British Columbia royalty. North America's largest Chinese restaurant offers 20,000 square feet of dining and seats 1,000 guests; its bustling ambience whisks you away to the heart of China for an hour or two's exhilarating adventure. Sponsor of the Chinese New Year Parade and Chinatown Festival, Floata is the creative force behind community events, where it offers up its award-winning culinary wonders.

The restaurant arrived on the Vancouver scene in 1996 and continues to serve up many surprises that satisfy the most daring palate in traditional Chinese style. Whether catering to dinner for two or a special event for hundreds, the restaurant presents an elegant atmosphere with mouthwatering Chinese fare that is world-class—the popular restaurant has locations in Hong Kong and 20 establishments in Shanghai, Beijing, Tianjin, and Macau.

400-180 Keefer Street, Vancouver
604.602.0368 www.floata.com

Photographs by Brian Yu

GRANVILLE ISLAND BREWING

Canada's first microbrewery, Granville Island Brewing began brewing beer in 1984 under the Bavarian Purity Law, which only allows four ingredients: malt, hops, yeast, and water. The Canadian-owned brewery currently strives for innovation in beer styles because the West Coast consumer is adventurous and willing to push the envelope on new and unique flavors. Made on-site and with all-natural ingredients and no preservatives, the beers are still brewed in basic adherence to the Purity Law but occasionally with the addition of such natural flavors as raspberry, honey, and ginger.

Located near the entrance to Granville Island in a building that was once a textile mill and still has cranes in the rafters from the old days, the brewery also offers beer tastings and education about the brewing process and has a beer and wine store. The brewery's relaxed atmosphere and tasting room provide the perfect venue for functions, events, and parties. With a well-established name in British Columbia, the beers are found in many local restaurant chains and offer the perfect way to wind down after a day of skiing, biking, or sightseeing.

1441 Cartwright Street, Vancouver
604.687.2739 www.gib.ca

Photographs by Jennifer McGreggar, Granville Island Brewing

HANDI CUISINE OF INDIA

Feast your eyes on Amar Maroke's tantalizing menu and you'll know that variety is the spice of life. A tempting array of traditional homemade dishes proves his passion for rarefied flavors from the long-forgotten frontiers of India. At the age of 12, Amar moved from India, eager to work in his family's restaurant business spanning three generations. After several years of cooking, he was inspired to become a professional chef. In 2005, with credentials in hand, he realized his dream by founding Handi Cuisine of India on Dunbar Street, a bistro-style restaurant specializing in award-winning fine East Indian cuisine. Amar insists that every Handi chef come from his native homeland, ensuring the cultural authenticity of each heavenly morsel prepared in their busy kitchens. Even the restaurant's moniker, Handi, refers to the traditional, thick-bottomed clay pot with a narrow-mouthed neck used for lengthy simmering, producing rich and deeply spiced tastes true to India.

With a talented team of servers and chefs who believe in absolute perfection, a dining experience at Handi reaches new heights of satisfaction, appealing to all five senses. Aromatic, colorful, and enchanting entrées include succulent kebabs drenched in flavorful Indian spices, sizzling tandoori, savory curries, house signature dishes, vegetarian specialties, fresh-baked naan, and sweet desserts. Deliciously exotic cuisine pairs nicely with a sophisticated beer and wine list to enhance your dining experience, while generous portions and attractive prices make Handi a hotspot for relaxing dinners and lively group parties in a genuinely friendly atmosphere.

Handi Cuisine of India has a creative, contemporary ambience, and the cozy romantic bistro on Vancouver's Westside has led to the opening of a chic waterfront restaurant with a spectacular ocean view patio and private dining room. The restaurant serves all of Vancouver and was voted "The Best of the City" by Westender, Vancouver's *Urban Weekly*.

4432 Dunbar Street, Vancouver
604.738.3186 www.handiwestside.com

Photographs by JulianOnePlanet Technical Photography

INTO CHOCOLATE SPECIALTY SWEETS

Craving fine chocolate? Get your fix on historic Glover Road, where fellow chocophiles have discovered a little bit of heaven. As you enter Into Chocolate Specialty Sweets shop, the aroma of cocoa beans wafts through the air, a familiar scent so innocently alluring and decadently delightful it tantalizes your senses. Professional chocolatier Delaine Willms had a delicious dream: She wanted to create a European, country-style sweet shop where chocolate connoisseurs and candy lovers of all ages could satisfy their desire for the best. An array of artisan confections is beautifully presented in the windows of her quaint cottage storefront, tempting all to indulge in a seductive sweet any time of day. More than 30 different types of filled and flavored Belgian chocolates—including high cocoa content, single origin, and rich molded pieces—star on the menu. "Create Your Own Collection" invites customers to choose a special gift box and handpick favorites for the ultimate customized treat. Owners Delaine and partner-husband Doug welcome new guests and bask in their guilty pleasure of offering a beautiful assortment of artisan chocolates and confections that are "unabashedly sweet," the charming shop's catchy slogan.

Whether you're in the mood for chocolate "shotz" or pure cacao with healthy antioxidants, Delaine and Doug are there to make your taste-tempting adventure complete. Like a friendly bakery café, there are always sweet samples to savor. Weekend events include wine-and-chocolate pairings that bring wine enthusiasts and chocoholics to a state of sweet inspiration. But there's more than gourmet chocolate to entice. The shop has British bon-bons, spicy licorice, a connoisseur corner, nostalgia candies, nutty fudge, and crunchy brittle, as well as unique party novelties and wedding favors. The sweet shop's passionate owners have even perfected a recipe for authentic "drinking chocolate" originating from the elite ancient Mayan culture, a dark chocolate elixir known for its rejuvenating powers, intense taste, and smooth texture. Nestled in the small village of Fort Langley, the family-owned sweet shop offers a truly transformative experience, creating melt-in-your-mouth smiles and happy feelings all around.

9217 Glover Road, Fort Langley
604.882.7317 www.intochocolate.ca

Photographs by Cole Vineyard

Kreation Artisan Cake

During the four years the Canada Line public transit system was under construction, a lot of businesses located along Cambie Street suffered. But when your business sells Earl Gray chocolate mousse cake, lavender shortbread, and blueberry tarragon tarts—all enhanced with real fruit instead of chemicals or food coloring—you don't suffer so much as thrive.

Kreation Artisan Cake is the result of a skiing accident that left hotel baker and former fine arts–jewelry design student Kaeko Kanno unable to work for two years. While recuperating, Kaeko began making wedding cakes and eventually needed more space, fulfilling a dream of owning her own bakery. Her husband Shawn and children Elina and Isao all contribute, making Kreation truly a family business.

Besides the row upon row of delectable goodies available in the store, Kreation also designs spectacular event cakes. Gum paste flowers are a particular specialty for weddings, but these cakes can and do feature everything from intricate, scrolling mehndi designs to silky iced peacock feathers. The Vancouver Opera and Science World have both displayed Kreation cakes at their special events. And if the event being celebrated is nothing more than a regular Tuesday afternoon, green tea and chestnut cake or milk chocolate pear mousse make more than adequate substitutes.

3357 Cambie Street, Vancouver
604.871.9119 www.kreationartisancake.com

Photographs courtesy of Kreation Artisan Cake

La Piazza Dario Ristorante Italiano

In the inspiringly beautiful town of Sorrento, Italy—around the bend from the famed Amalfi Coast, a short sail from the isle of Capri, about 20 miles from historic Pompeii—chef Claudio Ranallo got his start. He enrolled in culinary school at the tender age of 15 and trained with prominent chefs in Italy, Switzerland, and Canada.

The same year that Vancouver's Italian Cultural Center opened, 1977, Claudio realized his lifelong dream of establishing a restaurant that embodies his rich heritage: a picturesque setting and a hospitable culture centered on delectable cuisine made with farm-fresh ingredients. He and

his wife Lidia are the proud owners of La Piazza Dario Ristorante Italiano, which boasts an inviting Mediterranean ambience and offers a true taste of Italian goodness. Insalata di mare, fettuccini alla bolognese, tiramisu, a bottle of imported wine, and the company of friends or family all make for a fabulous evening.

3075 Slocan Street, Vancouver
604.430.2195 www.lapiazzadario.bc.ca

Photographs by Jessica Ranallo

THE MARINA RESTAURANT

Showcasing the province's finest regional ingredients from land and sea, Victoria's legendary Marina Restaurant is locals' destination of choice. Adding to the appeal are its surroundings of sparkling views of the bay with a mélange of masts and sails, the straits of Juan de Fuca, and postcard-perfect panoramas of Washington's volcanic Mount Baker.

The restaurant invites patrons to discover fresh-from-the-Pacific culinary delights, unsurpassed finesse of service, and incomparable ocean views.The talented executive chef blends the freshest produce and fish into imaginative creations, designs seasonal dishes with earthy rainforest mushrooms, whips up delicious creamy clam chowder, grills wholesome Arctic char, and bakes an array of sumptuous pastries. The Marina Restaurant boasts an ever-changing menu of innovative French-influenced and West Coast-inspired entrées and an extensive regional and international wine list. Whether offering diners creative fare at Sunday brunch, palate-awakening flavors in a masterfully prepared dinner, or the irresistible allure of an exquisite first course with a celebratory sip of cellared Dom Perignon, the restaurant makes Oak Bay Marina a requisite port of call for every Victoria voyage.

1327 Beach Drive, Victoria
250.598.8555 www.marinarestaurant.com

Photographs courtesy of The Marina Restaurant

MILANO BOUTIQUE COFFEE ROASTERS

Searching for a blend of West Coast heart and Italian soul? This rare combination of taste and artistry does exist. From original founder Francesco Curatolo's dream to Linda and Brian Turko's inherited passion, the couple's Vancouver coffee bar has become a legendary landmark for locals and visitors alike. Those who share an enthusiastic desire for true Italian artisan coffee—espresso the way it was meant to be—can enjoy eight exciting blends of premium Arabica coffee bean varietals. Master roaster Brian Turko has a trademark slow-roasting ritual and recipe that creatively combines select seeds for distinctive flavor and aroma that discerning coffee drinkers know and love. Roasting all of their coffees on site, the family-run business has a very organic approach, maintaining high Old World standards. The perfect roast profile with a balance of body, flavor sweetness, acidity, and aroma is achieved; the result is a truly unique coffee experience.

Coffee snobs unite. Milano Boutique Coffee Roasters is a place to hang out and sample the best espresso this side of Milan's bustling café row, where each day after 5 p.m. chic urbanites go on a café crawl. Just like visiting Milanese bars and cafés with their addictive atmosphere, coffee house buffs have discovered Vancouver's answer to the international espresso scene. That's exactly what Milano Coffee possesses with its intoxicating scent of fresh-roasted beans in the air and perky conversation all around. Three generations of Italian heritage blended with a quarter century of West Coast coffee culture culminate in Milano Coffee's world-class Italian espresso and exotic coffees. A relaxed ambience, the European-style pastry shop, and tempting panini menu complement Milano's sleek coffee bar and allow guests to sate their palates and enjoy an amazing view of the mountains and an awesome deck for socializing. The owners' commitment to authenticity with fresh forward-thinking honors centuries of hand-crafted coffee tradition with a decidedly trendy touch. Buon appetito!

156 West 8th Avenue, Vancouver
604.879.4468 www.milanocoffee.ca

Photographs: top and bottom by Mark Mushet; center by Victor Chew

SECTION (3) RESTAURANT

In 1994, Salli Pateman opened a 30-seat bistro called De Niro's in a forgotten area of the city known as Yaletown. It was an abandoned industrial area, but Salli had a vision of creating a funky hideaway for locals where the food was simple, fresh, and delicious, the atmosphere was sexy and laidback, and the cocktails were shaken—not stirred. Her tiny hole-in-the-wall soon attracted a diverse and dynamic crowd, from struggling screenwriters and actors to celebrities and entrepreneurs. In 1999 Salli made headlines when Robert De Niro sued her for using his name under Section (3) of the BC Privacy Act.

Fast-forward to the present. Yaletown is now one of the hottest neighborhoods in Vancouver, and although Salli's original bistro is now Section (3) Restaurant, a 150-seat mainstay of the urban restaurant scene, it still feels like home to the legion of regulars who continue to dine at her table. The old adage "locals know best" is still true today, and although Yaletown has changed dramatically, her simple philosophy of taking care of people has not.

In a world of copies, Section (3) is a true original. It's obvious from the moment you step inside. Seek refuge in an authentic place where you can enjoy locally sourced menu items, an old-fashioned cocktail, or a glass of wine, and relax and be yourself. You're in Sal's place, and she takes care of her friends.

1039 Mainland Street, Vancouver
604.684.2777 www.sectionthree.com

Photographs: top by Malcom Perry; bottom and facing page by Cameron Pashak

197

GRAY MONK ESTATE WINERY

The oldest family estate winery in British Columbia, Gray Monk Estate Winery is a cultural institution indeed.

George and Trudy Heiss, originally hairdressers from Edmonton, Alberta, had been growing grapes for 10 years on their Okanagan vineyard before deciding to open a winery. Believing the vinifera grapes of their land could yield top-quality wines, Gray Monk Estate Winery opened its doors in 1982. Their instincts were right, and today the property encompasses a store, seasonal restaurant, and—of course—winery tastings and tours year-round.

With George and Trudy's three sons involved in the business—Robert in operations, George Jr. in winemaking, and Steven in sales and distribution—this is truly a family legacy. Everyone is dedicated to crafting consistently high-quality, flavorful, fairly priced wines and presenting them in a manner that is welcoming, educational, and memorable. Gray Monk takes great pride in selling wines grown and bottled right in British Columbia, and lays a unique claim to fame. If the Tuscan-style winery building with a clay tile roof and arched entryways framed by incredible views of Okanagan Lake don't convince you of that, the superb hand-crafted wines paired with the delectable cuisine at the Grapevine Restaurant will.

1055 Camp Road, Okanagan Centre
250.766.3168 www.graymonk.com

Photographs: left by Brian Sprout; bottom center by Stuart Bish; bottom right by Robert Heiss; top right by Stuart Bish

NK'MIP CELLARS

On the fringes of a wild sage desert there lives a magical place. For many years the Okanagan reservation had ranching and farms on its land, the livelihood of Aboriginals in this southernmost region. The Osoyoos Indian Band has a thriving history here and winegrape growing is one recognized specialty they have acquired. The band cultivated vines on 340 acres at the NK'Mip Vineyard, first planted in 1968, producing fruitful yields every year due to the geological bench's longer sun-drenched days and cool nights. In 2002 the Osoyoos Indian Band and Vincor opened NK'Mip Cellars, a destination estate winery that speaks to its agricultural legacy.

The first Aboriginal-owned winery in North America now grows new varieties of grapes to create a diverse portfolio of wines. NK'Mip Cellars produces pinot blanc, riesling, chardonnay, pinot noir, merlot, cabernet sauvignon, syrah, riesling icewine, and a red blend called Meritage. Grapes are harvested exclusively from the Inkameep Vineyard—which operates under viticulturist Sam Baptise—and a 1,200-acre vineyard site. Passionate winemaker Randy Picton crafts distinctive vintages that have

earned more than 100 medals since 2002, creating pure expressions of the terroir and fully embracing the winery's mantra: "Discover the legacy of our land in every glass." NK'Mip Cellars was an addition to the multimillion-dollar Spirit Ridge Vineyard Resort & Spa, expanding Osoyoos Chief Clarence Louie's vision of achieving self-reliance for his people. Chief Clarence's dream inspired the luxury resort-winery complex with its award-winning architecture, superb suites and villas, The Patio restaurant, Cultural Centre, Sonora Desert Spa, and Sonora Dunes golf course. You'll be lured by its enchanting beauty—as a refreshing lakeside oasis amid the only pocket desert in Canada, some consider it to possess the most spectacular views in the Okanagan. It's all underscored by the fascinating tribal heritage and wine tastings to quench the thirst and please the palate.

1400 Rancher Creek Road, Osoyoos
250.495.2985 www.nkmipcellars.com

Photographs courtesy of NK'Mip Cellars

Okanagan Spring Brewery

Gold. Black. Copper. Brass. These distinctive colors sound like descriptions of precious metals and rich minerals from deep in the earth. But these are color scale hues of a popular thirst-quenching liquid: beer. One of British Columbia's original craft breweries, Okanagan Spring was founded by Buko von Krosigk and Jakob Tobler, two men from Germany determined to offer an alternative to the local mainstream beers.

Where better to pursue this goal than in a region marked by natural beauty and a history of fine brewing? Established in 1985 and brewing from the same location today, the Okanagan Spring Brewery resides in the fertile Okanagan Valley. Surrounded by mountains amid the beautiful Kalamalka and Okanagan Lakes, it's the perfect place to brew a variety of all-natural craft beers. Okanagan Spring beers are made in small batches using four pure ingredients: barley, hops, yeast, and spring water. And, according to the Bavarian Purity Law of 1516, this is all it takes to make a savory brew characterized by freshness and full flavor with absolutely no additives. Buko and Jakob didn't realize the role that Okanagan Spring would play in popularizing craft brewing, but they did know they'd created a mighty tasty beer. Regular favorites include Pale Ale, 1516 Bavarian Lager, Porter, Brewmaster's Black Lager, Hopped Lager, and summer and winter Craft Packs. Here, have a beer!

2808-27 Avenue, Vernon
250.542.2337 www.okspring.com

Photographs by Subplot Design

SUMAC RIDGE ESTATE WINERY

The Okanagan Valley has become known as a breathtakingly beautiful premium grape-growing region. This glacial land boasts mineral-rich soils, attracting vignerons from around the world, but it was a local who discovered its fruitful secrets first. Sumac Ridge Estates Winery is the oldest operating estate winery in British Columbia, founded in 1979 by Harry McWatters. A visionary winery proprietor and founding director of the British Columbia Wine Institute, Harry created one of the most renowned winery experiences in Canada, recognized for his passion, innovation, and commitment to quality. While he no longer runs the winery, the team's dedication to producing world-class wines in a relaxed, unpretentious setting remains. It's all about having fun. This is a place where guests happily adopt the winery motto: "Celebrate every day, pop the cork, and enjoy some bubbles."

Perched on a rocky knoll in Summerland with views of orchards, vineyards, and Okanagan Lake, Sumac Ridge sources abundant grapes from acreage in an ideal climate. The southern Okanagan Valley area enjoys long sunny days and extended growing seasons. Cultivating superior grapes, Sumac

Ridge became one of the first Canadian producers of "liquid gold" icewine and the introducer of Meritage, a complex Bordeaux blend. The illustrious winery produces pure varietals including a broad range of cool-weather whites and reds: Gewürztraminer, merlot, cabernet sauvignon, chardonnay, and cabernet franc. Talented winemaker Jason James harvests each varietal at optimal ripeness according to the wine it is destined for; he has traditionally handcrafted award-winning vintages since 2005 at Sumac Ridge. Then there are ever-popular table wines, sparkling wines, and dessert wines, with many derived from the Black Sage Vineyard designation. Wine lovers of all levels are invited for a tour and a sampling of new vintages in the cozy tasting room, Chef Fuller's latest wine pairings at the Cellar Door Bistro, or a glass of dry white on the patio while gazing at gorgeous hillsides.

17403 Highway 97, Summerland
250.494.0451 www.sumacridge.com

Photographs courtesy of Sumac Ridge Estates Winery

Kids Market, page 228

The Dog & Hydrant, page 218

Maiwa Handprints, page 233

The North Face Store by ECO Outdoor Sports, page 240

Hudson Madison, page 226

body politic, page 210

Panache Antiques and Objets d'art, page 243

MCL Motor Cars, page 235

SHOP

BOUTIQUES & SHOWROOMS

Glance. Browse. Attain. Shopping in British Columbia is an experience like no other. You've got an all-access pass to some of the finest boutiques and showrooms nationwide, with something new to find around every corner. Gift shops, jewelry stores, home décor boutiques, electronics stores, public markets, and shopping centers are all available for your perusal. Whatever you're seeking—music, fashion, furniture, specialty groceries, even pet supplies and luxury automobiles—it can be found in BC.

JORDANS

Jordans' history dates back more than eight decades to the Great Depression when Edwin Jordan-Knox founded the business, primarily for the sale of Oriental rugs, on Vancouver's Granville Street. His goal was to bring to Western Canadians the finest pieces from Persia, China, and India, and to do that with integrity. Regardless of the vast changes that have occurred in the industry since then and the expansion of Jordans to 38 locations and multiple products and services, the core beliefs of the employees still match the original focus on values and commitment.

Today, Jordans continues to be family-owned and operated, and has expanded to offer every item essential to creating a fabulous space—from superb furniture, draperies, and accessories to fashionable, beautiful floor coverings from around the world. Each store reflects its surrounding area, disregarding the one-size-fits-all rationale and instead celebrating the uniqueness of the people within the neighborhood or region. With a focus on color, texture, design, and quality—the foundation for an outstanding room—experienced interior designers and expert flooring consultants are dedicated to continuing the company's long history of credibility and dependability.

1470 Broadway, Vancouver
604.733.1174 www.jordans.ca

Photographs courtesy of Jordans

Photographs courtesy of Jordans

BASQUIAT

Historic Yaletown has developed quite a reputation for excellent quality in its retail shops, and Basquiat is no exception. Opened in 2005, Basquiat is the combined effort of a pair of lifelong friends, Cristina Linden and Liselott Montesano. Having both worked in fashion for decades, Cristina and Liselott combined their knowledge into a fashion boutique to clothe stylish trailblazers in the latest design trends.

At Basquiat, every line is hand-selected from an international roster of fashion icons, such as Ilaria Nistri, Willow, and Vivienne Westwood. Shopping exclusively for their clientele, the fashionistas find themselves in Italy, France, and North America, painstakingly searching for the perfect items. Liselott even designs an exclusive line of jewelry. Basquiat is a large, spacious, inviting shop that offers limited, individual in-house consultations—a personal touch deserving overwhelming kudos from Basquiat's patrons.

1189 Hamilton Street, Vancouver
604.688.0828 www.basquiat.ca

Photographs by Jeff Vinnick

BLUSHING BOUTIQUE

Seasonal fashion shows, monthly wine-and-cheese parties, and—of course—an ever-changing selection of Shelley Klassen originals: Blushing Boutique is the Vancouver hotspot for ladies who appreciate timeless couture presented in a chic, approachable setting. Dresses are the designer's passion, so the boutique offers a grand variety of day, cocktail, and evening frocks, as well as stylish separates just right for both daytime and special occasions. Custom-made garments are de rigueur for those wishing a perfect fit, and alterations and fittings are done in-house too. Shelley loves to see how her creations complement various body types and hear how each piece makes a woman feel. She takes the feedback to heart and uses it to perfect works in progress and inspire future collections.

The design diva's career officially started during her undergraduate years, when fans of her exceptional wardrobe became her first clients. Such early success propelled her to hone her talents studying haute couture at an Ottawa fashion design academy.

Shelley's method is unique: Fabrics come first because their color, pattern, and texture dictate how the design will unfold; each finished work of art is fresh, dazzling, and perfectly detailed. All of Blushing Boutique's designs are made in the heart of Vancouver—many are sewn at the attached atelier and design studio—and showcased on-site. Select shops across North America also carry Shelley's classic creations.

579 Richards Street, Vancouver
604.709.3485 www.blushingdesigns.com

Photographs courtesy of Blushing Boutique

BODY POLITIC

Sometimes it's all about being in the right place at the right time. When Nicole Ritchie-Oseen decided to open a clothing boutique showcasing reclaimed materials and sustainable design, she knew Vancouver would be the perfect place to set up shop. The city's progressive attitude and eclectic, independent vibe mirrored her proposed boutique body politic's earth-friendly and stylish vision. Inspired by her mother's encouragement to make her business ethical, Nicole has been selling "eco-fashion" in the hip and vibrant Main Street neighborhood since 2008. The boutique focuses exclusively on North American designers, and the fashion-forward styles are made from materials such as organic cotton, soya, hemp silk, jersey, and even a beech wood fiber known as modal. Recycled gold, silver, leather, and other salvaged bits and pieces are born again into jewelry and accessories.

Reclaimed vintage and antique furniture and energy-efficient lighting highlight the funky space. Teeka, Nicole's friendly little Havanese pup, can often be found touring the store. The dog's enthusiasm for greeting shoppers is matched by her owner's desire to surprise people with cutting-edge fashions, courtesy of independent designers from Vancouver to New York. The shop proves you can have sustainable design with limitless style.

208 East 12th Avenue, Vancouver
604.568.5528 www.bodypolitic.ca

Photographs by Ed Araquel, model Bobbi B. for Lizbell Agency

BONERATTLE MUSIC

Upon entering Bonerattle Music, visitors won't find solemn piano music or an intimidating atmosphere. Instead, both the novice and professional musician, and even the casual passersby, will walk into a comfortable setting in which testing instruments or breaking out in impromptu jam sessions are both common and highly encouraged.

Phil Addington, who opened the shop in 2006 after leaving supermarket management for a change of pace, has always loved music. As the bass player in a cowboy punk band, he realized his neighborhood lacked a music shop and saw the opportunity to encourage a love of music in others.

Bonerattle's welcoming ambience allows curious children and professional band members alike to relax and find just what they need. There's no shortage of unusual instruments, intriguing percussion-type noisemakers, and high-end guitars to try a beat or two on.

In addition to the variety of musical equipment, the shop provides instrument repairs by the well-known Graeme Pattison. And if learning to play a note is on the to-do list, Bonerattle can help in that area too. Private lessons in guitar, bass, mandolin, and steel guitar are offered by musicians with international reputations.

2012 Commercial Drive, Vancouver
604.251.2663 www.bonerattle.com

Photograph by Eugenia Filippova

CITY SQUARE SHOPPING CENTRE

Two granite and sandstone buildings, featuring stained glass windows, a copper cupola, and slate roofs, were built in 1905 and 1908 to house the teaching-related Model School and Normal School. The structures found another purpose in 1989 when they became the foundation for City Square Shopping Centre, a well-rounded mix of offices, shops, and services that also serves as a meeting point and social center for the people of Vancouver.

Located in the heart of the Cambie community and across the street from Vancouver City Hall, City Square has delivered what the area lacked previously—a space where people can converge as well as connect. Doctor's offices, two grocery stores, a salon and spa, and fitness and yoga centers are only a sampling of the ways City Square is helping its neighbors conduct a healthy, satisfying daily lifestyle.

Each year, among other community involvement events, City Square organizes the Halloween Hunt, a free event with family-friendly trick-or-treating, games, and entertainment. A popular jazz festival turns City Square into a free venue for people to enjoy themselves and the music, while the Emergency Preparedness Fair seeks to educate the community and provide the public with pertinent information from industry leaders on disasters.

Architect Paul Merrick was the catalyst for this sense of community by designing the retail storefronts to resemble a streetscape, with ceiling skylights and old-fashioned lamp posts. The center's interior emulates a series of small open-air courtyards. The resulting effect has the ambience of a European village mixed with the bustle of urban life.

555 West 12th Avenue, Vancouver
604.876.5165 www.mycitysquare.com

Photographs by David Priban

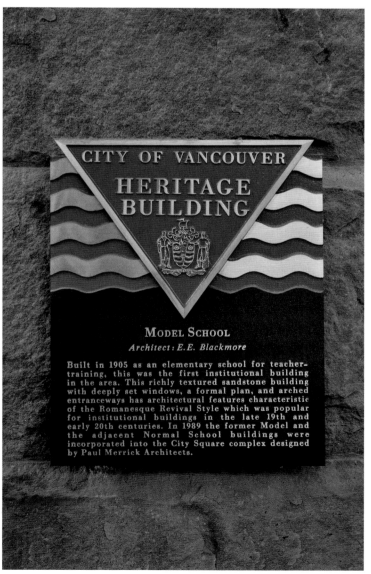

CITY OF VANCOUVER
HERITAGE BUILDING

MODEL SCHOOL
Architect: E.E. Blackmore

Built in 1905 as an elementary school for teacher-training, this was the first institutional building in the area. This richly textured sandstone building with deeply set windows, a formal plan, and arched entranceways has architectural features characteristic of the Romanesque Revival Style which was popular for institutional buildings in the late 19th and early 20th centuries. In 1989 the former Model and the adjacent Normal School buildings were incorporated into the City Square complex designed by Paul Merrick Architects.

CHARALS

There is an understated luxury to the business professional who has made it. This is not just the subtle elegance of classic sartorial details, but also the accoutrements to the business lifestyle. This is total attention to detail: the perfect pen for the writer, the perfect accessory for the businessman, the truly unique and extraordinary.

For more than 20 years, Charals has been offering the highest quality gifts and accessories for accomplished professionals. Cartier, Montblanc, Tumi, Porsche Design: Here pens, wallets, briefcases, luggage, desk accessories, journals, cards, and Filofax organizers seem to reinvigorate style and elegance to a market once thought lost to the world of disposables.

For Al Charania and his wife Shelina, Charals is the family business and much more—a demonstration, in fact, of the family's vision of the best of the best. As an ambassador of the finer things in life, Charals turns its waterfront location into a fascinating dive into the trimmings of the modern professional: One location, worldwide.

Suite 222-757 West Hastings Street, Vancouver
604.689.3497 www.charals.com

Photographs by Al Charania

COMMERCIAL DRIVE BUSINESS SOCIETY

If you wander a few minutes from downtown, on foot or via transit, you'll soon find yourself walking along Commercial Drive. And before you know it, you'll experience the essence of a unique community with all your senses—taste, touch, sight, and more. As Vancouver's expressive edge, it's a place beloved by locals and travelers, and a community that truly is one-of-a-kind.

Commercial Drive is a fantastic mix of traditional and trendy. It's alive with artistic expression, and rich in history and cultural diversity. As Vancouver's "Little Italy," it houses some of the best gelato, cappuccino, and delicatessens in the city. The Italian heritage is part of a multicultural mosaic, creating an eclectic community known as "the Drive." Within this urban playground spanning 21 blocks, there are 200 merchants that encompass live music venues, shopping, dining, indoor art displays, and an outdoor art gallery of expressive murals.

From cool vintage stores and fashion boutiques to European-style cafés and organic grocers—and ethnic restaurants to satisfy any craving—Commercial Drive welcomes you to discover it!

1726 Commercial Drive Suite 4, Vancouver
604.251.2884 www.thedrive.ca

Photographs courtesy of Commerical Drive Business Society

COUNTRY BEADS

In October of 1994, Sue Gill opened the doors to Country Beads. Artistic and creative with a background in graphic design, she wanted to make the craftplace that she wanted to go to but couldn't find; being a social person, she also wanted to nurture a social environment. Country Beads is a shop where people can gather and create, a place full of row upon row of jars and vials like a colorful apothecary. The hands-on staff teaches and assists, offering beading classes and personalized attention, empowering people to take pride in their creativity, and helping them to craft the perfect piece of jewelry for any special occasion.

Since the company's opening day, the merchandise mix has expanded to include an extensive selection of semiprecious stones in a multitude of shapes, from smooth to hand-cut facets. Thus the shop has evolved into a worldly guild for eclectic, elegant, and sophisticated craft—appealing to a range of people from fashion jewelers to up-and-coming artists and designers. Every culture adorns the body, so the beads come from every country—beads made from recycled bottles in Africa, South American ceramic beads, and glass beads from Europe. The beads serve many functions: they can be used as jewelry or accessories; they can decorate clothing. After all, virtually anything can be turned into a bead.

2015 West 4th Avenue, Vancouver
604.730.8056 www.countrybeads.com

Photographs by Trish Connolly, Katwalk Photography

THE CROSS DÉCOR & DESIGN

Just as in "The Sound of Music," Stephanie Vogler and Darci Ilich surround themselves with a few of their favorite things at The Cross Décor & Design, a 1914 building transformed into 5,000 square feet of shopping heaven. A wonderland of lifestyle accessories, the store showcases everything from bedding to bath, sofas to scented candles, and ribbons to wrap—even designers and personal shoppers are available.

The owners' backgrounds and talents are an ideal combination. Stephanie's entrepreneurial spirit was embedded by her parents, while Darci's love of design led her to excel with display suites. Together they created The Cross, so named because of its strong connotation yet varying meanings.

Located in the trendy Yaletown area, the shop's inviting ambience allows visitors to wander a maze of treasures amid an amazing sensory experience. Romantic music, delicious smells, occasional tea tastings, and knowledgeable staff encourage shoppers to explore every nook and cranny so they, too, can find their favorite things.

1198 Homer Street, Vancouver
604.689.2900 www.thecrossdesign.com

Photographs by Janis Nicolay Photography

The Dog & Hydrant

Hundreds of happy families owe their adoption success stories to Tanya King, pet photographer extraordinaire. But residents of Vancouver Animal Shelter are not the only ones who benefit from Tanya's artistic savvy. With equal parts patience and creativity, she also does commissioned portraits, capturing the unique personalities of dogs, cats, and rabbits—she's even photographed a parrot—against a crisp black or white background. Tanya credits her visual storytelling skills to commercial advertising photographer Hans Sipma, but she's clearly developed an appealing style all her own.

Tanya's trendy Yaletown studio, The Dog & Hydrant, doubles as a pet merchandise and treat boutique—the gigantic freezer full of doggie delicacies is a requisite stop with every visit. From collars, leads, and clothes to toys and grooming supplies, the boutique has a great selection of locally made and specially imported gear that is functional, not too frilly, and fun.

Whether stopping by The Dog & Hydrant to pick up a few canine necessities, have a photo shoot, attend the semiannual Fleas Knees fundraiser, or meet Saturday's dog to adopt, patrons and their pets are delighted with the boutique's high-quality offerings and wonderful pet-friendly atmosphere.

1146 Pacific Boulevard, Vancouver
604.633.3845 www.thedogandhydrant.com

Photographs by Tanya King

FINE FINDS

At the start of the century, Fine Finds first opened its doors as a furniture boutique, and it has since transformed into one of the Yaletown heritage district's premier fashion destinations. Fashionistas and followers alike regularly flock to the exclusive store's prime location in the heart of Yaletown, where truly fabulous finds abound. A huge selection of handbags and jewelry is dwarfed only by the eclectic, ever-changing mixture of fashionable clothing available.

Founder Jane McFadden along with partner Megan Maxwell scour the globe, scrutinizing every product that crosses their path. Only those that will dazzle the imaginations of their customers make it into their inventory. With such dedication to clientele and savvy discretion, it's no wonder the award-winning store attracts the attention of chic shoppers all over Vancouver.

1014 Mainland Street, Vancouver
604.669.8325 www.finefindsboutique.com

Photographs by Richard Bernardin

FITNESS TOWN

After more than 20 years in the fitness industry, James Newman felt the call to help more people reach their health goals. In 2006, he and business partner Dai Manuel opened the first location of Fitness Town in Burnaby as a specialized showroom offering quality fitness equipment and accessories. With the subsequent opening of seven additional locations—six in British Columbia and one in Edmonton—James and Dai continue to advance the importance of long-term health and fitness.

The company encourages BC and Alberta residents to engage in a lifestyle many are already prepared for—after all, according to Ipsos Reid a little over half of them report having at least one type of fitness equipment in their home, ranging from free weights to a treadmill to a stationary bike. Accordingly, each Fitness Town location offers a wide range of equipment, including everything from home gyms to ellipticals to vibration technology. Yet the equipment isn't even Fitness Town's greatest asset; the knowledge and expertise of the associates make the difference. Taking into account the goals each person has in mind, the staff works to find the right fit for the individual, showing each patron how to best utilize the equipment. So whether it's with a new piece of equipment, helpful educational materials, or just encouragement to pursue a personal goal, James, Dai, and their team hope to enhance the lifestyles of those in the surrounding communities.

4141 Lougheed Highway, Burnaby
604.299.7716 www.fitnesstown.ca

Photographs courtesy of FitnessTown

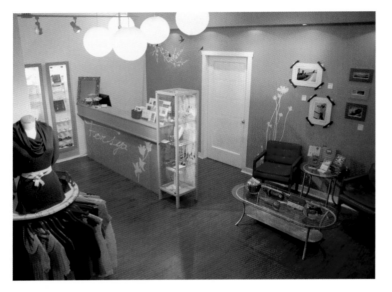

FORSYA BOUTIQUE & GALLERY

Offering edgy designs of clothing, jewelry, and accessories for the young urban professional, Forsya Boutique & Gallery is in a class of its own.

Julie Hebb, a visual artist, designer, and animator, opened the boutique to support local artists and independent designers across Canada—all of the store's designs, including about a dozen lines of jewelry, are designed and made in Canada. Julie, coming from a long line of shop owners and having apprenticed with a fashion designer, had always wanted to own a boutique. With the support of her husband Keith, she opened the store on Vancouver's bustling Main Street in 2009.

The airy boutique doubles as a gallery and is filled with not only cutting-edge clothing designs but also extraordinary art showcasing established and upcoming artists. Locals and tourists alike enjoy browsing and learning the interesting stories behind each creation. The origin of the boutique's name? "Forsya" is fondly adapted from Julie's beloved granny's name.

2206 Main Street, Vancouver
604.568.8667 www.forsyaboutique.com

Photographs by Julie Hebb

FOSTER WALKER

A socially and environmentally responsible enterprise, Mardi Foster-Walker's privately owned shop is committed to green living, and a portion of its profits goes to support charitable and nonprofit organizations. Beyond benevolence and a visionary approach, her showroom (by appointment only) focuses on Canadian-made products, supporting local artists and manufacturers while promoting beautiful luxury goods and contemporary artifacts intrinsic to the cultural heritage of the Pacific Northwest and British Columbia.

The Foster Walker gift gallery has been in business since 1989, carrying exclusive custom-made and Canadian-born giftware from personalized premiums for business events to indigenous Inukshuk sculptures, one of the Vancouver 2010 Winter Olympic Games symbols. "May the Inukshuk be your guide for a safe journey throughout life's travels," is one of the company's mantras. Jade, finely cast bronze, soapstone, wood, and other natural materials are hand-carved by local artisans and find their way to Foster Walker's shelves, ready to enchant shoppers. Art glass, cast paper sculpture, original photographic images of Vancouver, and native silver and gold etchings by Bill Reid are just a few of the fantastic collectibles available. Foster Walker is a veritable guided tour of Canada's fine arts and crafts as well as unique gourmet selections. And if you're looking to put a logo on a Canadian-inspired gift—from a mountain hiker's knapsack to a sophisticated wine set—Foster Walker represents more than 1,000 lines of merchandise appropriate for customizing.

Suite 303-1230 Haro Street, Vancouver
604.681.2456 www.fosterwalkergifts.com

Photographs by Ron Sangha

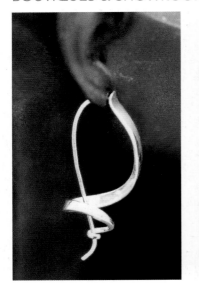

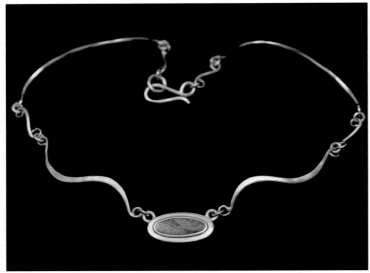

HÉLÈNE BOURGET DESIGNS

Forming 18-karat gold, bright platinum, and pure silver into wearable art is Hélène Bourget's forte and great passion. Creating in her Vancouver studio, she transforms precious metals into rings, bracelets, earrings, and pendants that are at once original, sensitive, and breathtaking. Hélène handcrafts her metalwork jewelry designs, often layering yellow gold with gleaming silver, artfully integrating finely cut diamonds, colored gems, semiprecious stones, and rare pearls to express a concept of her own, or that of one of her discerning patrons.

Hélène Bourget Designs symbolize love, happiness, and the beauty of life; each sculptural piece exudes emotion and epitomizes sophisticated adornment. Her alchemy begins in the studio, where she sketches original concepts and brings them to life through traditional silversmith methods and age-old goldsmithing techniques. Inspiration may come directly from nature, yet it is often her freshly imaginative ideas that manifest into stunning creations. Hélène works to suit the individual wearer, always pushing her comfort zone, reaching higher to make pieces that have never before existed. She is a visionary jewelry designer who shares nature's raw gifts from deep in the earth by bringing elegant pieces to life through her innate creativity. Celebrities, brides and grooms, and lovers of quality craftsmanship desire Hélène's contemporary jewelry, appreciating her sense of authenticity and urban-chic style. Eclectic in her artistic approach from "concept to creation," Hélène's handmade jewelry has been exhibited in museums and is frequently featured in the media. Hélène is a purist who immerses herself in all aspects of the design process, and a visit to her studio will truly inspire you.

Vancouver
604.669.5925 www.helenebourgetdesigns.com

Photographs by Hélène Bourget

HOUSEWARMINGS

A home is a place to relax, to feel comfortable, to rejuvenate. For Briar Codesmith, everyone should be able to feel this sense of home and appreciate their surroundings. This ideal has inspired Briar toward two related passions—a lifelong interest in charities for the homeless and her more recent endeavor of HouseWarmings, a home décor boutique.

With a focus on making a house a home at HouseWarmings, Briar selects furniture, home décor, accessories, and jewelry that embrace everything from whimsical to functional, fashionable to classic. Realizing that basic investment pieces are the building blocks for a great room, Briar often showcases neutral furniture with accessories that pop with color. Her appreciation for organic items spills over into the store, too. Items such as wine bottle holders carved from natural rocks are often in stock, as are bulk packages of seeds, pods, and twigs, always a popular section.

HouseWarmings isn't just a place to shop for décor; it's a warm, inviting atmosphere where guests find design inspiration. Briar's unique presentation receives compliments for the interesting pairings and brilliant placement. And with an ever-changing feature wall that reflects current trends, outstanding style is always at guests' fingertips.

14016 32nd Avenue, South Surrey
604.535.6554 www.housewarmingsdesign.ca

Photographs by Carol Stoller

HUDSON MADISON

Transforming homeowners' dreams into reality is Susan Teschke's passion. Proprietor of the interior design shop Hudson Madison, she shares her talent by offering an exclusive collection of home furnishings for forward-thinking clientele with an admiration for hand-crafted quality and chic design. "I select timeless transitional pieces that will enhance a home environment today, yet are destined to become the next generation's antiques," says Susan. Hudson Madison's broad selection of sophisticated sofas, chairs, tables, sideboards, and lighting fixtures are handmade by Canadian fabricators and artisans, especially local craftsmen. The shop carries clean-lined pieces that can easily go traditional or contemporary, depending on your desired design approach, wood finish, color scheme, or fabric choice. For instance, Hudson Madison's signature Hedley dining table can look decidedly hip, yet has a classic structure for more traditional room settings.

The Hudson Madison philosophy is clear: Interior design should be a personal interpretation and true extension of self. Whether you want full design services for a new home construction project or simply need help selecting a proper paint color, the talented staff focuses on guiding your decisions to truly reflect who you are. Those who want to know where style is going visit Susan's trendsetting shop to get new ideas and indulge their wish for a more beautiful home. Beyond fine furniture, the Abbotsford boutique also presents an exciting gallery of unique art, décor, gifts, window treatments, and seasonal items, in an atmosphere of chic tranquility that invites you to linger. Since the concept store's debut in 2004, Hudson Madison has steadily grown to become Western Canada's premier interior decorating and design resource, with new locations popping up all across North America.

101-2031 McCallum Road, Abbotsford
604.853.1404

Photographs by Jo Balisky

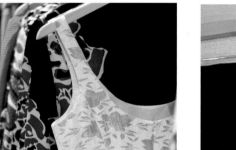

ISHARA

Equipped with two graphic design academy and business school degrees, Amrit Baidwan dreamed of having an urban-chic design company and fashion boutique. With sights set on creating a fashion playground for women, she opened the ultimate closet in Gastown, deemed by the media as Vancouver's place for fashionistas and high-style professionals. The inspiring boutique's moniker, Ishara, means to send someone in the right direction, and the sophisticated destination boutique draws tourists and locals alike with its hip atmosphere. The store is the cool culmination of the owner's heart's desire coupled with her eye for au courant, luxurious style.

The exclusive clothier is a place where people can mingle amid well-chosen racks of contemporary designer garments, accessories, and jewelry. Display window mannequins don LA labels and New York brands along with select pieces from Paris that quietly lure shoppers inside its modish walls. One-of-a-kind designs, premium denim, and celebrity-quality pieces hang like paintings in an art gallery, ready for savvy shoppers to try new looks and play dress-up from Amrit's handpicked collections. Ishara associates work closely with guests, much like personal image consultants, to assist in selections that will enhance their individual beauty and style. Ishara shoppers each walk away with an original look and own it, making haute fashion statements that reflect their unique personalities.

38 Water Street, Vancouver
604.264.7494 www.shopishara.com

Photographs: top, center, and bottom left by Lauren Keogh; top, center, and bottom right by Kevin Wongosaputra; top center left by Kevin Wongosaputra; top center right by Lauren Keogh; bottom center by Kevin Wongosaputra

KIDS MARKET

Founded in 1984, Kids Market is not just a shopping experience but an adventure focused on children. Providing services such as hair cuts—including baby's first hair cut—birthday parties, a two-story play area, an arcade, and rides, the entertainment complex is often mistaken for a department store, but it is really a collection of individual boutique shops and activities.

The shopping mall is unique in North America and offers products from costumes to kites to clothes, toys to treats to magic tricks, and a variety of weekend activities like crafts, ceramics, and sand art. Christmas becomes a child's dream come true when Santa not only meets them but also reads to them and plays and sings with them.

The building, formerly a paint factory, took two years to transform into one of Granville Island's most recognizable buildings with a bright yellow exterior. Primary colors paint the building's interior, which features such novelties as an extra small kid-sized entry door and sinks, a wall of water, and other points of interest to induce sensory overload—every inch is designed to delight and inspire play and imagination.

1496 Cartwright Street, Vancouver
604.689.8447 www.kidsmarket.ca

Photographs: bottom right courtesy of Vancouver Public Library Archives; all others by Eric Milner

KIU SHUN TRADING COMPANY

Wandering the packed shelves of Kiu Shun Trading Company is a bit like stepping into another land entirely. Apothecary-style jars and bins of exotic foodstuffs, ginseng, tea, nuts, fruit, and more crowd the aisles, emanating an aromatic scent. This is more than a mere Asian imports shop—this is an old-fashioned health food store rooted in traditional Chinese herbology.

Established in 1977, by owner Albert Fok's father, the enterprise—the first of its kind in Western Canada—represents the fourth generation of a family business begun in mainland southern China more than 130 years ago. Albert, born in Hong Kong and raised in Vancouver, is the perfect embodiment of traditional Chinese upbringing uniting with the 21st century. Nestled in the heart of Chinatown in Vancouver—a city known as the Asia Pacific gateway—the store is uniquely positioned to take full advantage of that cultural melding. Signs throughout the store are in English, French, and Chinese, and the qualified, expert staff all speak

English too. Queen Elizabeth of England has even awarded Albert with a Medal of Distinction for community contribution.

The shop prides itself on providing only the best quality items—Albert is aware that because people purchase these items for health maintenance, they must be of the highest caliber. Traditional Chinese herbal formulations are preventative rather than curative, connected to regular and natural diet practices above all, and the store with its knowledgeable staff—including certified traditional Chinese medicine doctors—and attached acupuncture clinic reflects that dedication to holistic healthcare for all patrons.

261 Keefer Street, Vancouver
604.682.2621

Photograph by Albert Fok

LuxSalon European Bathrooms

When it comes to home design, bathrooms are considered equal with kitchens in terms of the importance we place on atmosphere, materials, and fixtures.

LuxSalon European Bathrooms caters to those seeking the best in bathware, supplying patrons with everything needed for a bathroom in one location. The business is Vancouver's exclusive distributor of Royal Sphinx sanitary ware imported from the Netherlands. The showroom's selection of wall-mount, height-adjustable washbasins, toilets, and bidets is continually expanded with new offerings from respected designers such as Antonio Citterio and F.A. Porsche.

LuxSalon focuses on European-inspired bathroom solutions that make the most efficient use of space and enhance ease of maintenance. The retailer promotes "wet rooms," a barrier-free, open-space shower environment featuring a linear drain seamlessly integrated into the tile floor.

For those who appreciate the quality and streamlined design of European-crafted products, a visit to LuxSalon is a must.

192 West 3rd Avenue, Vancouver
604.707.9131 www.luxsalonbathrooms.com

Photographs courtesy of Royal Sphinx

LOLO JEWELLERY & ACCESSORIES

Childhood entrepreneurs often grow up to become business-savvy professionals, and designer Lorena Ponis, the mastermind behind Lolo Jewellery & Accessories, is no exception. After all, it should come as no surprise that a budding industrialist who sold cookies in school at the age of eight, was peddling the hair accessories she created from silk scarves to local salons by high school, and pursued a travel-intense international business career now finds herself the center of an expanding jewelry and accessories enterprise.

Lorena's drawn to the creative industry because she gets a thrill out of creating—or discovering—objects and seeing people enjoy using them. In 2003 she founded her own design line, Lolo, named after Lorena's nickname. Through Lolo, Lorena combines her creativity with a passion for fashion by designing jewelry for women, especially brides, and her lines have been a huge hit thanks to her adherence to a simple yet successful formula: classic, versatile jewelry fit for any occasion. The pieces utilize only the finest materials—like Swarovski crystals, semiprecious stones, and high-quality silver and gold—and the resulting designs are stunning. Lolo's bridal selection, quite popular, is incredibly expansive, and a selection of leather handbags is slated to debut as well. Lolo is growing rapidly, and Lorena and her skilled staff—including production manager Taryn Tyrrell, instrumental to the process—are more than ready to handle it.

Appealing to an international clientele, Lolo's designs are shown in boutiques across Canada and as far away as the UK.

604.937.8508 www.lolo.ca

Photographs: left by Gabrielle Beer; right by Evaan Kheraj

MAIWA HANDPRINTS

The vanishing art of handmade textiles has been gloriously revived, thanks to the passion of Charllotte Kwon from Maiwa Handprints on Granville Island. Founded in 1986, Maiwa supports traditional craftspeople in the production of embroidered, block printed, hand-woven, and naturally dyed textiles from many countries, especially India. Inside The Net Loft shop, the Maiwa staff educates visitors about the culture of each garment or artifact and shares information about the co-op and living conditions of represented artisans. "Every thread has a story," says Charllotte. Her annual Maiwa Textile Symposium ties the artisan community together even further and works to raise awareness about international textiles through scholarly lectures and films.

So indigenous cultures may flourish, Maiwa pursues a rare business model that demands trust between artisan and entrepreneur. The process begins much like commissioning artwork: Artisans are advanced on a large order, and as segments of the order are filled, complete payment is made. Because Charllotte believes that the survival of any culture depends on the aesthetic freedom of its people, she never dictates pattern, color, or motif. She encourages detailed and elaborate work, knowing that the exquisite beauty of a skillfully produced design will attract buyers and positively benefit the artist's livelihood and village. In a world economy where mass-produced clothing is commonplace, the quality of life for each "slow clothes" artisan comes from respect earned as a master craftsperson. Maiwa Handprints beautifully showcases artisans' original, handmade textile designs, which are born of unbridled creativity and pride of craft.

6-1666 Johnston Street, Vancouver
604.669.3939 www.maiwa.com

Photographs: top left and right by Tim McLaughlin; center by Tim McLaughlin; bottom by Sophena Kwon

MCL Motor Cars

MCL Motor Cars of Vancouver offers some of the finest luxury vehicles in the world by offering the ultimate in design, performance, comfort, and service. The European imports dealer has been a vibrant presence in the city for over three decades, offering a high standard of service befitting each marque— Aston Martin, Bentley, Jaguar, Land Rover, and Porsche, all of which combine legendary artistry with excellence in engineering. Clientele is composed of an eclectic mix of elite entrepreneurs, established professionals, entertainers, international royalty, and loyal car enthusiasts—and all are treated as valued, longtime patrons. When a new model is introduced, the dealership presents the debut vehicle in a celebratory atmosphere for all those in the MCL family to enjoy.

MCL's storied past and bright future as a leader in luxury vehicles is incomparable. Its three dealership locations share the belief and philosophy of continuous improvement in products, value, human relations, teamwork, and industry competitiveness. The showroom's astute automobile experts go out of their way to provide a satisfying experience. They've established connections to the quality brands that exemplify elite status while fulfilling every car aficionado's passion for driving well-engineered, handcrafted vehicles. The dealership ensures that each vehicle meets rigorous standards, so that all vehicles are not only works of art but also provide each customer with a supremely enjoyable ownership experience.

MCL Motor Cars
1730 Burrard Street, Vancouver
604.738.5577 www.mclmotorcars.com

Porsche
1718 West 3rd Avenue, Vancouver
604.736.7911

Aston Martin
1820 Burrard Street, Vancouver
604.733.1820

Photographs courtesy of MCL Motor Cars

Mona Euro Furniture

The transition from Iran to Germany to Vancouver may not be obvious for most people, but for Mona Euro Furniture founder Mohammad Ali Ahmadpur, the move was a no-brainer. Born in Iran with a passion for amazing furniture, Mohammad first opened a high-end furniture retail location in his home country; he moved to Germany in 1985 to open a second location. Realizing the opportunities to bring the high-end European furniture to other countries, he sought out Vancouver for its ethereal aspects and its diverse culture.

In a stunning 30,000-square-foot downtown showroom, manager Stan van Woerkens keeps a variety of designer pieces in stock, including unparalleled Himolla and Rolf Benz designs. With a focus on elegance for a lifetime, the laid-back European styles offer great sightlines for those who appreciate luxury. Also within the showroom are opulent European bedding ensembles to bring numerous concepts for the entire home together under one roof. Mona Euro Furniture is also home to friendly and knowledgeable staff who are not pushy or pretentious, but offer service and intriguing stories to match the high-end quality of the designs.

With one step inside Mona Euro Furniture, it's evident why Mohammad had to share these remarkable designs with North America.

142 Water Street, Vancouver
604.684.6662 www.monaeurofurniture.ca

Photographs: top and center by Rolf-Benz; bottom by Himolla Polstermöbel; facing page by Rolf-Benz

New Objects of Desire

Striking a wealth of great design is the ultimate experience for the chic, modern shopper, and Nood—New Objects of Desire—brims over with original and innovative treasures. The hip retro and modern furniture will add character and flair to any room while a great mix of fun décor and gifts for the kitchen, homeware, bed, and bath—bamboo towel sets, sleekly designed accents, and even quirky pieces like a yellow duck toothbrush holder—will add splashes of taste and fashion to your home.

With plenty of great gift ideas, Nood encompasses a range of fun and well-designed products that permeate style. From furniture, ceramics, and luggage to gadgets and home textiles—and just about everything in between—all Nood products are designed to be stylish and contemporary while casual and comfortable.

The eclectic product categories create an element of adventure and discovery for patrons. Offering a new level of accessibility and affordability to well-designed and beautiful lifestyle and homeware products, Nood aims to satisfy the style requirements of discerning shoppers looking to surround themselves in little luxuries.

151 Water Street, Vancouver
604.684.9008 www.noodDesign.ca

Photographs by Kristen McGaughey

THE NORTH FACE STORE BY ECO OUTDOOR SPORTS

Living in British Columbia may predetermine a person to live an active lifestyle and love the outdoors. After all, residents are surrounded by nature so wild and abundant that exaggeration becomes impossible. You would be hard-pressed to find other places on earth where you could ski in the morning, kayak in the afternoon, and cap off the day with a relaxing rock climb. Immeasurable opportunities for adventure follow naturally.

After years of outfitting people heading into the outdoors, ECO Outdoor Sports started a new venture with one of the most reputable and respected brands in the outdoor industry, The North Face. In 2006 the firms opened their first single-brand partner store in Vancouver, offering top-flight clothing and equipment for any type of excursion. This was followed in 2009 by a new flagship The North Face Store in the heart of downtown Vancouver.

No matter what type of patron enters—a mountaineer looking to be outfitted for Everest, a hiker searching for the perfect camping gear, or a visitor needing a waterproof jacket for a stroll in the lush BC rainforests— knowledgeable employees strive to satisfy every request. The ECO Outdoor Sports philosophy of "Love life actively" embodies the core value of The North Face: "Never stop exploring."

2136 West 4th Avenue, Vancouver
604.677.6269 www.ecooutdoorsports.com

Photographs: top and bottom courtesy of The North Face; center left by Tim Kemple; center right by Jimmy Chin; facing page by Mark Synatt

PANACHE ANTIQUES AND OBJETS D'ART

There's a treasure hunt going on at Vancouver's Panache Antiques and Objets d'art. Sometimes the prize is a Dutch masterpiece, an antique Russian icon, or a Chinese ceramic piece. Perhaps, if your timing is just right, an early American William and Mary chest. For Joan Bilchik, the hunt has been going on since 1986, when she opened Panache in South Granville's culture-rich Gallery Row.

Originally from South Africa, Joan uses her extensive experience and training in art history, design, and material culture to handpick pieces for her shop from her eclectic array of antiques. Her keen eye has even discovered items of historical and artistic significance. Joan welcomes inquisitive shoppers and seasoned connoisseurs alike, and if your tastes lean to furniture, silver, textiles, or tole glass lighting, she will delight in revealing the history and story of each object with obvious passion. Panache also specializes in the consulting, appraising, and brokering of fine art and antiques, but it's the instant gratification of making shoppers happy that inspires Joan to continue her hunt.

2212 Granville Street, Vancouver
604.732.1206 www.panacheantiques.com

Photographs by Fred Granzow

THE PERFUME SHOPPE

Fragrance stirs the soul, the emotions, the senses. What every woman wants is a signature scent, one that inspires images of beauty, romance, and love. An original fragrance is intoxicating to the wearer and alluring to others with its elusive quality. Exotic essences, when combined using the right chemistry, emanate flavors and smells of flowers and spices found in nature. One touch of precious fragrance on the skin can transport us. Fragrance often marks a moment in time. We tend to be drawn to familiar scents that evoke fond memories.

The Perfume Shoppe in Vancouver's Sinclair Centre is an exquisite fragrance boutique founded by proprietors Naz and Amyn Ladha—the duo also has an Arizona location. Their hundreds of perfumes include hard-to-find scents and exclusive luxury brands such as Amouage, Carthusia, Clive Christian, Comme des Garçons, L'Artisan Parfumeur, Lorenzo Villoresi, Montale, Parfumerie Generale, Penhaligon's, and Serge Lutens. Entering the perfumery is a transformative olfactory experience. Naz was born in Zanzibar, commonly referred to as the Spice Islands, and is blessed with a keen sense for fine fragrance. There's an aura about her; she learned the craft from her father, which has led to her lifelong passion. Having worked with haute European perfumeries, Naz is an expert who guides visitors to that perfect fragrance creation. "The personality of perfume should be as individual as the wearer," says Naz. Perfume is a stimulant of the senses, a balm for the spirit. High notes can be exciting, sensual, mysterious, calming, or fresh—the possibilities are endless.

Suite 226-757 West Hastings Street, Vancouver
604.299.8463 www.theperfumeshoppe.com

Photographs courtesy of The Perfume Shoppe

PILAR'S BOUTIQUE

Pilar Buse knows what's hot and what's about to be. When she's not traveling the world to discover fabulous new clothing lines, Pilar is keeping tabs on the ever-evolving fashion industry and preparing user-friendly seasonal trends reports from her eponymous boutique.

Raised in Peru by a widowed mother who was busy with a family of eight, Pilar developed both a strong sense of determination and a love of fashion at a young age. From carefully redesigning hand-me-down dresses as a little girl to currently developing her own line of premium yet highly approachable clothing as an entrepreneurial woman, Pilar has a wonderfully rich perspective to share with Western Canada. She and her fashion-forward team love to help gals of all ages find the perfect look for their body types and aesthetic sensibilities, but they are equally content to stand by to answer questions or provide feedback. Whether researching, designing, styling, or giving back to the community through youth outreach and other organizations, Pilar believes in doing everything with love.

B5-940 Main Street, West Vancouver
604.925.0426 www.pilarsboutique.com

Photographs by Sugar Creative

ROMANCING THE HOME

Romancing the Home has created a charming ambience to entice the discerning shopper. Although immediately apparent to passersby, the allure intensifies with one step inside the home décor and gift store and ensures a return visit, if for no other reason than just to catch another glimpse of the delicious eye candy on display. Whether looking for a distinctive piece of jewelry, a locally crafted gift for a special someone, or a sophisticated décor item to enhance your home, Romancing the Home is the perfect place to find that desired gift.

First opened in 2004 by Jill Martyniuk, whose background spans everything from the corporate world to the artistic, the shop boasts an eclectic collection from both local artisans and worldwide sources. Exclusive pieces, like locally crafted furniture, Sid Dickens Tiles, and jewelry by Myka and Thomas Sabo, are displayed next to luxurious bath and body lines, beautifully boxed dish sets, and adorable baby gifts—all with the common theme of top-notch quality. Propelled by a passion for finding unique items for the discerning shopper, Jill takes cues from the surrounding community when choosing items and in creating a comfortable feel within her classy boutique. Everyone from the young to the young at heart will enjoy the ever-changing mix that keeps the shop fresh and inviting.

1637 128th Street, Surrey
604.542.9600 www.romancingthehome.ca

Photographs by Julian Price

247

ROXANN'S HATS

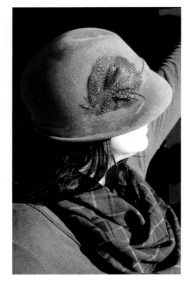

Alice in Wonderland's Mad Hatter would be proud. Roxann's Hats is a Fort Langley institution that has been making heads turn since 1998. The Gasoline Alley millinery boutique is a hat fanatic's dream where shoppers can play, experiment, and transform themselves just by trying and buying a new hat. Founded by Roxann McKamey, the store has an enchanting ambience. Roxann is a lover of fashion and the arts, raised by a mother who always wore a hat and brought Roxann to the milliner's with her, so she channels her love of artistic expression into her shop to stimulate the fashion senses of all who enter. The walls, racks, and countertops are brimming with hundreds of imaginative hats reflecting Roxann's vibrant philosophy and zest for life and all things beautiful.

Browsers and hat buffs strolling along the boutique-lined streets are lured by the shop's funky, comfortable atmosphere. Inside, every surface is blanketed with hats, hats, and more hats—plus a few scarves, handbags, and other accessories. Some styles have movie star connections, from well-made fedoras inspired by infamous characters in *The Godfather* to ladylike chapeaus reminiscent of those worn by Hollywood icon Audrey Hepburn. Fancy themes, fetish designs, fashion statements, and unadulterated fun describe the array of amazing hats in Roxann's handpicked collection. Guests can relax, model their favorite hat in the mirror, and laugh together as everyone gets the chance to play dress-up—and perhaps waltz out the door with a new hat.

9203 Glover Road, Fort Langley
604.882.8077 www.roxannshats.com

Photographs by Julian Price

SINCLAIR CENTRE

Step into the past—walk out with the latest look. Destination shopping is what it's all about at Sinclair Centre, the vibrant downtown district's elite boutique complex, housed in four heritage buildings built in the early 1900s, exhibiting the opulent Edwardian Baroque revival style. Painstakingly restored in 1986 to bring back its original character, the 66,000-square-foot complex has been transformed into a sophisticated shopping mall and beautiful atrium, including a busy tower of government offices and services. A classical quartet of structures, from the 1910 post office to the handsome Winch Building circa 1911, the Customs Examining Warehouse built in 1913, and the Federal Building completed in 1937, Sinclair Centre is one of Vancouver's most photographed landmarks. But it's the outstanding, high-end shopping experience that local urbanites and visitors are powerfully drawn to, with dozens of world-class stores amid the architecturally esteemed walls.

The original post office building catches your eye with its English and French influences, and the atrium's 12-foot-diameter clock circa 1909—with the largest clock movement in Western Canada—reminds you that it's the perfect time to shop. All-the-rage retail names dominate this downtown architectural gem. Sinclair Centre touts extraordinary designer brands in the numerous boutiques lining its historic hallways, as well as local shops you can only browse in Vancouver. Sip lattes in its charming café, have a quick bite in the food court, and be stopped in your tracks by creative window displays at L2 Leone, Castle Milano, Charals, Leone Boutique, The Perfume Shoppe, Diamond Deals Jewellery, and Escada, to name a few.

340-757 West Hastings Street, Vancouver
604.488.0672 www.sinclaircentre.com

Photographs by Daniella Wray

249

Showcase Pianos

Sheer genius. Beautiful to behold, delightful to hear, and amazing to play. Putting your fingers to the keyboard of a finely crafted piano is like touching the steering wheel of a Ferrari, whether you play pure jazz, pop, or classical. There's a bit of magic in a fine piano. From painstaking Italian craftsmanship to heavenly tone and responsiveness, discerning enthusiasts agree, there is nothing better than an instrument that intuitively knows what to do, bringing your performance to life through every single key.

Owner Manuel Bernaschek has a passion. As a piano lover who recognized the need for fine pianos in Vancouver, he founded Showcase Pianos in 2007. Showcase Pianos carries only the finest artist's instruments, highlighting world-class Fazioli and Grotrian brands. But it was the Fazioli piano that inspired Manuel the most. For many years there was much talk in the piano community about a man in Italy who was making the finest pianos in the world. "We kept hearing that more and more famous pianists were converting to playing on Fazioli pianos, so I really wanted to bring them here," says Manuel. He was determined to introduce one of the greatest concert grands in the world to his talented locale, handmade by world-renowned Paolo Fazioli. The German-made Grotrians are another notable draw. Over the past several years, Showcase Pianos has made a name for itself serving exquisite instruments of music to cherish and enjoy, with a crescendo of acclaim that resounds throughout Vancouver's most illustrious private homes and concert halls. Bravo!

1224 West Broadway, Vancouver
604.437.5161 www.showcasepianos.com

Photographs: top and bottom by Leo Cai; center by Scott Adolph; facing page by Scott Adolph

SPIRITHOUSE

Spirithouse takes you on an exquisite tropical journey that will leave you entranced and engaged. This fair-trade bazaar showcases the wonderfully exotic colors and textures of Thailand that inspire all who travel there. The store's flagship product, the teakwood spirit house, represents spiritual harmony and balance and plays on the imaginations of young and old alike. Teak furniture and décor made from salvaged farm equipment and timber speak of a uniquely Thai creativity and ingenuity. Drape yourself in sumptuous silks, explore ethnic fashion, or browse myriad gifts. Happiness and beauty radiate throughout the store to leave you healed and inspired.

To owner Uli Rasehorn, Vancouver—known as the gateway to Asia—is a natural market for the high quality art, craft, furniture, and fashion he selects during his travels. A social entrepreneur, Uli takes pride in supporting a thriving, sustainable cottage industry that provides incomes to villagers. With the immense worldwide interest in meditation and yoga, Thai culture and style appeal to our inner search for spirituality and simple, natural living. Spirithouse takes shopping to a new dimension that is at once exciting and deeply rewarding.

3673 West Broadway, Vancouver
604.730.8310 www.spirithouse.ca

Photographs by Julian Price

THE TA DAA LADY

Oral storytelling is one of the oldest art forms; in fact, it was an essential mode of transmission in passing down history and knowledge. While the medium of communication differs today from what was available in the past, the art of creative, compelling storytelling remains the same.

Angela Brown has taken that art and molded it into unique children's entertainment—a perfect convergence between distilling important information and having delightful fun. With many years of performing artistry in her background and a love for working with kids, Angela quickly agreed to friend and fellow performance artist Evelyn Roth's idea to truly engage her young audiences with her Nylon Zoo creations.

Evelyn's designs—hand-sewn, three-dimensional kinetic sculptures and costumes—supply the perfect props for Angela's interactive performances. Centered on diversity and environmentally friendly themes, each story tells a fascinating legendary tale about an animal or spirit. The performances begin with a costume parade and dance, with a story and songs following inside the large inflatable creation. Each audience member, complete with a costume, becomes part of the event for an unprecedented storytelling experience.

66506 Summer Road, Hope
604.649.1979 www.angelabrown.ca

Photographs: top by Casey Mons; center and bottom by Tom Tasse

Taraxca Jewellery

Window shopping in the trendy-chic Kits neighborhood is great, but a visit to Taraxca Jewellery's design gallery of gleaming and frosted sterling silver, stainless steel, gemstone pieces, and one-of-a-kind artisan creations is absolutely unforgettable. Inspired on their road trip to Mexico after an earlier journey to Nepal, Melissa and Hector Aragón brought back a car full of silver jewelry they found in quaint villages where artists craft sterling into fabulous forms. The Taraxca proprietors are adventurous travelers eager to share rare artistry the world has to offer; she's an anthropologist with a passion for history, he's a computer scientist with an eye for innovation. It's no wonder that their eclectic boutique has become a mecca for jewelry lovers with a penchant for the unique.

You don't need a passport to discover handcrafted silver from Mexico, golden amber from Poland, volcanic sea-blue larimar from the Dominican Republic, polished semiprecious stones from Brazil, sparkling gems originating from Thailand and India, and unique designs made by British Columbia's talented local artists. Taraxca Jewellery has locations in Tsawwassen Quay Market, Vancouver International Airport's domestic terminal, and the avenues near downtown. Every necklace, bracelet, or pair of earrings has a story, but their true beauty is reflected in the eye of the beholder. Taraxca's timeless designs follow one rule: simplicity and quality. Handcrafted pieces possess organic shapes and figures of stunning beauty, suitable for all ages and discerning tastes. Exotic shell, wood, and pearl creations made of natural treasures are also part of the complete Taraxca collection. The art of adornment is ages old and Taraxca brings new forms of feminine allure in its array of contemporary expressions. This is jewelry at its finest, inspired by nature, destined to be worn by every woman.

1834 West 4th Avenue, Vancouver
604.732.8990 www.ilovesilver.ca

Photograph by Grant McAvoy, Image Werx Photography

Nature's Fare Markets

Many modern grocery stores are saturated by profoundly unhealthy, dubious quality foodstuffs lining the shelves. A store committed to organic foods, responsible supplementation, and a holistic lifestyle is a breath of fresh air indeed, and Nature's Fare Markets has filled that niche since 1981.

The concept was born when founder and owner Rick Monahan, disappointed by conventional grocery stores, decided to create a new kind of health-focused shopping experience that offers patrons a full selection of vitamins, supplements, and organic, locally sourced fare. This supplies health-conscious consumers with a shop that contributes to physical and mental wellbeing—and the chance to support a business committed to customer service, integrity, and preserving the planet.

The first Nature's Fare opened its doors in Victoria and quickly proved Rick's vision a success. When he decided to move back to his hometown of Vernon and realized there was a shortage of natural food stores in the Okanagan region, the small Kelowna Orchard Plaza location opened soon after in 1994—and has since grown into the company's flagship store. The since expanded location features a large selection of natural groceries, an extensive vitamin department, organic produce, health and beauty aids, and The Apple Organic Bistro.

Today there are seven Nature's Fare locations throughout British Columbia, each populated by talented, dedicated, and knowledgeable staff—and each a socially and environmentally friendly place to shop.

101-4201 25th A Avenue, Vernon
800.406.6646 www.naturesfare.com

Photographs courtesy of Nature's Fare Markets

WESTCOAST AUDIO VIDEO GALLERY

Any audio-visual company that puts the word "gallery" in its name truly understands the importance of good design sensibility. That's what Robert Autar envisioned when he opened the doors to his Yaletown-based company in 2005: a store combining the most advanced, cutting-edge equipment with skilled technicians able to expertly disguise the products upon installation. Together with manager and client consultant Armand Rajkumar and head of installation and design Morgan McMillan, the team of three has grown the business to unimaginable heights.

Westcoast's motto—"Where Hi Performance Meets Designer Lifestyle"—is merely a prelude to the kind of work it produces. The young and energetic company marries its eye for contemporary style with absolute function, building a seamless transition between high-tech display and sophisticated subtlety. Its technicians specialize in meticulous attention to detail, helped along by formal education and a highly specialized tool arsenal. Vociferous recommendations from past customers fuel a strong word-of-mouth.

With the world growing more appreciative of high-end electronics every day, Westcoast Audio Video Gallery's place in both the residential and corporate markets is only expanding.

89 Smithe Street, Vancouver
604.669.5001 www.westcoastavgallery.ca

Photographs courtesy of Westcoast Audio Video Gallery

CS PrintMaster

Drawing inspiration from its stunning setting in Kelowna, CS PrintMaster produces amazingly beautiful products through its full-service commercial offset and digital printing facility. From impressive brochures to informative books to awe-inspiring postcards, the printed colors are just as vivid as in the surrounding landscape.

Since its beginning, CS PrintMaster was also prompted by the scenery to make a commitment to the environment. Through a production facility designed to make the smallest environmental footprint possible and the use of responsibly manufactured paper, the printing company strives to be a good steward of the natural elements so that future generations can continue to enjoy all that British Columbia has to offer.

Founded in 1985 by Sue Ranchie who was always interested in graphic design, CS PrintMaster has marvelously upheld its original mission: to offer quality, affordable printing for all businesses regardless of size. With a relaxed but professional atmosphere and a no-salesperson policy, Sue and her team—which includes a graphic design department and a full bindery service—treat every project with the same careful attention to detail and quality that keeps many satisfied customers coming back.

6A-1050 Leathead Road, Kelowna
250.491.4737 www.csprintmaster.com

Photographs courtesy of CS PrintMaster

FALCON WELDING PRODUCTS

Rather early in his career, Don Tansem earned the title of first-class journeyman welder. He enjoyed working with his hands and learning about the ever-changing welding industry trends and products. Ultimately, he decided to share his education and expertise in a different way and, with his wife Janice, entered into the welding supply industry, establishing WELDCO and then Falcon Welding Products nearly three decades ago.

Both companies quickly earned places at the forefront of the industry by developing strong working relationships with their welding shop clientele and being the go-to source for acquiring the latest technology—and information on how to maximize its potential. The businesses ushered in the use of high-tech MIG and TIG welders, introduced clients to plasma-cutting machinery, and revolutionized the houseboat industry in Kelowna by promoting water-cooled welding systems. As is natural with successful organizations, the companies branched out to also supply the region with

key industrial gasses, the uses for which are far more diverse than meets the eye. Professional welders, casual handymen, flower shop owners who sell helium balloons, bartenders serving up what's on tap, and doctors who rely on lifesaving medical gasses have all felt the influence of WELDCO and Falcon's presence.

In addition to bettering their native British Columbia through the success of their company, the Tansems have helped raise money for numerous medical research and youth outreach organizations, sponsored kids' sports team, served as presidents of local Kin Canada chapters and the Kelowna Boxing Club, and raised two sons to know the value of hard work and active community involvement. Now retired, Don and Janice live on beautiful Shuswap Lake.

Photograph by Jason Tansem

LENARCIC BROS CONSTRUCTION

A home is more than just a place to rest at night; it is a place where a group of people truly become a family, where life can be enjoyed. For brothers Mario and John Lenarcic, this sentiment was paramount to their decision to start Lenarcic Bros Construction in 1989. After working many years for other companies, the brothers decided to strike out on their own so they could ensure the resulting homes were just what each family needed. Over the past two decades, their goal has continued to focus on building high-quality houses that address the homeowners' needs. The team accomplishes this through its fabulous subcontractors as well as its hands-on approach. For example, despite the numerous years under its belt, Lenarcic Bros still does its own cribbing and framing.

What makes them truly stand out is their passion for British Columbia. Both Mario and John grew up in the Okanagan and still love the region. Kelowna's popularity as a four-season resort—with activities including everything from skiing to golfing and boating to camping—is just one of the many high points of living in the valley. Through each home the brothers build, they exude a thorough enjoyment of improving the community and helping families—whether young or old, first-time homebuyers, or seasoned residents—find a place to call their own.

3211 Vineyard View, West Kelowna
250.212.5755

Photographs: left by Lori Shaw Photography; facing page courtesy of Lenarcic Bros Construction

NAVIGATOR MULTIMEDIA

Greg Bauer knows how to seize an opportunity. In 1993, the internet was exploding in popularity and Greg, a veteran of the publishing and advertising industries, realized that businesses would be clamoring to establish a stable, professional web presence. Fast forward to the present, and Navigator Multimedia has grown into one of the foremost companies for web design, iPhone application development, online application programming and development, business class web hosting, search engine marketing, and graphic design.

With the help of IT manager Kirk Liu, creative director Chris Statterwaite, sales and operations manager Mike Thurstan, a dedicated staff of programmers and graphic designers, and Greg's wife Lynda, Navigator has developed many websites and online tools for local, regional, and provincial organizations. Tourism, entertainment, government, manufacturing, and viticulture are just a few of the market segments that have benefitted from the company's efforts. Greg and his team work hard to develop applications that help showcase the incredible province they live in, a place Greg describes as the best place in which to live, play, work, and raise a family.

Located in downtown Kelowna, just two blocks from the Cultural District and Lake Okanagan, Navigator also uses its community-oriented attitude to sponsor local organizations such as the Constable Neil Bruce Outdoor Education Program and the Central Okanagan Youth Soccer Association. Whether helping someone attract lucrative business deals or give their child more fresh air, Navigator Multimedia knows how to get the most from its opportunities.

201-260 Harvey Avenue, Kelowna
250.862.9868 www.navigatorweb.ca

Photographs by Jiri Bakala

Northern Log & Timber

Log home living exudes a certain ambience that is not felt with the building material of a conventional house. A log home imparts a sense of comfort, character, tradition, and style. It establishes a rustic and authentic feeling. With such unique distinction, a log home will be admired today and for years to come.

The more than 2,800 projects of Northern Log Homes have already been applauded for many years. With beautiful, charming homes that perfectly blend the historical tradition with today's living, not to mention the streamlined process and the elimination of common log-home construction issues, who could resist such a home? Northern homes are known for being cost efficient to construct, energy efficient to live in—costing 25 to 30 percent less to heat than a frame-construction home—and practically maintenance free, with the specially designed preservative that is applied to the exterior surface.

Since Northern's founding in 1952 by Al Morgan in the Yukon Territory, the log home has evolved dramatically. Over the years of logging, saw milling, and building homes, Al and his family have seen the raw log with bark morph into the round log system of today's handcrafted and kiln-dried machined log. Whether you're looking for a log or timber frame home, custom-cut timbers, or just drafting and design, the Morgan family will ensure the work is just what you need for log home living at its finest.

6-1050 Leathead Road, Kelowna
250.765.2408 www.northernlogandtimber.com

Photographs by Stuart Bisch

EXPERIENCE
BRITISH
COLUMBIA

BRITISH COLUMBIA TEAM

ASSOCIATE PUBLISHER: Marc Zurba
ASSISTANT PUBLISHER: Judith Walker
GRAPHIC DESIGNER: Kendall Muellner
EDITOR: Sarah Tangney
CONTRIBUTING EDITOR: Anita M. Kasmar
CONTRIBUTING EDITOR: Jennifer Nelson
CONTRIBUTING EDITOR: Lindsey Wilson

HEADQUARTERS TEAM

PUBLISHER: Brian G. Carabet
PUBLISHER: John A. Shand
EXECUTIVE PUBLISHER: Phil Reavis
PUBLICATION & CIRCULATION MANAGER: Lauren B. Castelli
SENIOR GRAPHIC DESIGNER: Emily A. Kattan
GRAPHIC DESIGNER: Paul Strength
MANAGING EDITOR: Rosalie Z. Wilson
MANAGING PRODUCTION COORDINATOR: Kristy Randall
PRODUCTION COORDINATOR: Drea Williams
PROJECT COORDINATOR: Laura Greenwood
TRAFFIC COORDINATOR: Katrina Autem
ADMINISTRATIVE MANAGER: Carol Kendall
CLIENT SUPPORT COORDINATOR: Amanda Mathers

PANACHE PARTNERS, LLC
CORPORATE HEADQUARTERS
1424 Gables Court
Plano, TX 75075
469.246.6060
www.panache.com

Vancouver Convention Centre, page 96

Steve Nash Foundation

The Steve Nash Foundation is a registered Canadian charity and 501(c)(3) organization formed to assist underserved children in their health, personal development, education, and enjoyment of life. Like its NBA MVP founder, the foundation is fast becoming a leader in assists—to a slightly shorter population.

Steve's homeland ties and deep appreciation for British Columbia's people, resources, and future drives his kinetic passion to help. In creating the Steve Nash Foundation, he recognized that giving children attention gives them opportunities: a chance to grow confidence and feel safe doing it, to learn about the world and all it can offer, and to develop health for a lifetime.

With supporters around the world, the Steve Nash Foundation is growing health in kids by implementing initiatives premised on the idea that children matter. With BC Grants, the foundation funds child-focused public service and nonprofit entities and projects that provide services to children affected by poverty, illness, abuse, or neglect, and create opportunity for education, health, and empowerment. Throughout the province, the foundation pursues creative, innovative projects that fill an observed need in a particular community. From the Sunshine Coast to its hometown in Victoria to East Vancouver to further east in Salmon Arm and north to Smithers, the foundation has bolstered capital and other projects that directly benefit communities' youth.

As corporations must share responsibility for the wellbeing of

communities, the foundation utilizes and encourages environmentally sustainable office practices, and assists grantees in developing their own energy conservation programs. The Steve Nash Foundation highlights the important work of other individuals and organizations, using its website and events to increase their exposure and contribute to their efforts. Further, it is proud to be working with young people who excel in their chosen fields: The foundation contracts for services with new companies and welcomes their energetic leadership and fresh voices.

The foundation also seeks to afford thoughtful solutions to community needs through its own platforms. Examples abound of the small yet dedicated staff's daily work: equipping Asunción, Paraguay's

Centro Materno Infantil with a post-operative pediatric cardiology ward; installing a pre-cancer screening and treatment clinic in Itauá, Paraguay; providing basic necessities for infants and their families through the Support Hope initiative; establishing the after-school Centre for Youth Assists in Toronto to build hope and leadership skills; bringing best practices in early childhood education and development to at-risk babies, toddlers, youth, and their families through Educare Arizona; providing cultural and reconciliation opportunities to war-affected communities of northern Uganda; restructuring child abuse prevention strategies to maximize integrative, sustainable outcomes for children across Canada and the United States; and uniting civic outreach, corporate, and social service organizations to get people involved in their

communities. Bringing research and critical needs resources to bear on the most vulnerable populations will alter trajectories, challenge outcomes, and change the world for the better.

Caring for kids means learning what they need and making sure that every child knows we care. Make the assist.

www.stevenash.org

INDEX

INDEX

Capilano Suspension Bridge, page 59

THE PANACHE COLLECTION

CREATING SPECTACULAR PUBLICATIONS FOR DISCERNING READERS

Dream Homes Series
An Exclusive Showcase of the Finest Architects, Designers and Builders

Carolinas	New Jersey
Chicago	Northern California
Coastal California	Ohio & Pennsylvania
Colorado	Pacific Northwest
Deserts	Philadelphia
Florida	South Florida
Georgia	Southwest
Los Angeles	Tennessee
Metro New York	Texas
Michigan	Washington, D.C.
Minnesota	
New England	

Spectacular Homes Series
An Exclusive Showcase of the Finest Interior Designers

California	Metro New York
Carolinas	Ohio & Pennsylvania
Chicago	Pacific Northwest
Colorado	Philadelphia
Florida	South Florida
Georgia	Southwest
Heartland	Tennessee
London	Texas
Michigan	Toronto
Minnesota	Washington, D.C.
New England	Western Canada

Perspectives on Design Series
Design Philosophies Expressed by Leading Professionals

California	New England
Carolinas	New York
Chicago	Pacific Northwest
Colorado	Southwest
Florida	Western Canada
Georgia	
Great Lakes	
Minnesota	

Art of Celebration Series
The Making of a Gala

Chicago & the Greater Midwest
Georgia
New England
New York
Philadelphia
South Florida
Southern California
Southwest
Toronto
Washington, D.C.
Wine Country

Spectacular Wineries Series
A Captivating Tour of Established, Estate and Boutique Wineries

California's Central Coast
Napa Valley
New York
Sonoma County
Texas

Specialty Titles
The Finest in Unique Luxury Lifestyle Publications

Cloth and Culture: Couture Creations of Ruth E. Funk
Distinguished Inns of North America
Extraordinary Homes California
Geoffrey Bradfield Ex Arte
Into the Earth: A Wine Cave Renaissance
Spectacular Golf of Colorado
Spectacular Golf of Texas
Spectacular Hotels
Spectacular Restaurants of Texas
Visions of Design

City by Design Series
An Architectural Perspective

Atlanta
Charlotte
Chicago
Dallas
Denver
Orlando
Phoenix
San Francisco
Texas

Experience Series
The Most Interesting Attractions, Hotels, Restaurants, and Shops

Boston
British Columbia
Chicago
Denver

Panache Partners, LLC   1424 Gables Court   Plano, Texas 75075   469.246.6060   www.panache.com